QUEEN VICTORIA

Deirdre Shearman

1986
CHELSEA HOUSE PUBLISHERS
NEW YORK
NEW HAVEN   PHILADELPHIA

SENIOR EDITOR: William P. Hansen
PROJECT EDITOR: John W. Selfridge
ASSOCIATE EDITOR: Marian W. Taylor
EDITORIAL COORDINATOR: Karyn Gullen Browne
EDITORIAL STAFF: Maria Behan
　　　　　　　Susan Friedman
　　　　　　　Pierre Hauser
　　　　　　　Perry Scott King
　　　　　　　Kathleen McDermott
　　　　　　　Howard Ratner
　　　　　　　Alma Rodriguez-Sokol
　　　　　　　Bert Yaeger
ART DIRECTOR: Susan Lusk
LAYOUT: Irene Friedman
ART ASSISTANTS: Noreen Lamb
　　　　　　　Carol McDougall
　　　　　　　Victoria Tomaselli
COVER ILLUSTRATION: Michael Garland
PICTURE RESEARCH: Tamara Fulop

Frontispiece courtesy of The Bettmann Archive

First Printing

Library of Congress Cataloging in Publication Data

Shearman, Deirdre. QUEEN VICTORIA

(World leaders past & present)
Bibliography: p.
Includes index.
　　1. Victoria, Queen of Great Britain, 1819–1901—Juvenile
literature.　2. Great Britain—Kings and rulers—Biography—
Juvenile literature.　[1. Victoria, Queen of Great Britain,
1819–1901.　2. Kings, queens, rulers, etc.]
I. Title.　II. Series.
DA557.S54　1986　　　941.081′092′4 [B] [92]　　　86-6796

ISBN 0-87754-590-1

Chelsea House Publishers

133 Christopher Street, New York, NY 10014

345 Whitney Avenue, New Haven, CT 06510

5014 West Chester Pike, Edgemont, PA 19028

Contents

ADENAUER
ALEXANDER THE GREAT
MARC ANTONY
KING ARTHUR
ATATÜRK
ATTLEE
BEGIN
BEN-GURION
BISMARCK
LÉON BLUM
BOLÍVAR
CESARE BORGIA
BRANDT
BREZHNEV
CAESAR
CALVIN
CASTRO
CATHERINE THE GREAT
CHARLEMAGNE
CHIANG KAI-SHEK
CHURCHILL
CLEMENCEAU
CLEOPATRA
CORTÉS
CROMWELL
DANTON
DE GAULLE
DE VALERA
DISRAELI
EISENHOWER
ELEANOR OF AQUITAINE
QUEEN ELIZABETH I
FERDINAND AND ISABELLA
FRANCO

FREDERICK THE GREAT
INDIRA GANDHI
MOHANDAS GANDHI
GARIBALDI
GENGHIS KHAN
GLADSTONE
GORBACHEV
HAMMARSKJÖLD
HENRY VIII
HENRY OF NAVARRE
HINDENBURG
HITLER
HO CHI MINH
HUSSEIN
IVAN THE TERRIBLE
ANDREW JACKSON
JEFFERSON
JOAN OF ARC
POPE JOHN XXIII
LYNDON JOHNSON
JUÁREZ
JOHN F. KENNEDY
KENYATTA
KHOMEINI
KHRUSHCHEV
MARTIN LUTHER KING, JR.
KISSINGER
LENIN
LINCOLN
LLOYD GEORGE
LOUIS XIV
LUTHER
JUDAS MACCABEUS
MAO ZEDONG

MARY, QUEEN OF SCOTS
GOLDA MEIR
METTERNICH
MUSSOLINI
NAPOLEON
NASSER
NEHRU
NERO
NICHOLAS II
NIXON
NKRUMAH
PERICLES
PERÓN
QADDAFI
ROBESPIERRE
ELEANOR ROOSEVELT
FRANKLIN D. ROOSEVELT
THEODORE ROOSEVELT
SADAT
STALIN
SUN YAT-SEN
TAMERLANE
THATCHER
TITO
TROTSKY
TRUDEAU
TRUMAN
VICTORIA
WASHINGTON
WEIZMANN
WOODROW WILSON
XERXES
ZHOU ENLAI

ON LEADERSHIP
Arthur M. Schlesinger, jr.

LEADERSHIP, it may be said, is really what makes the world go round. Love no doubt smooths the passage; but love is a private transaction between consenting adults. Leadership is a public trans- action with history. The idea of leadership affirms the capacity of individuals to move, inspire and mobilize masses of people so that they act together in pursuit of an end. Sometimes leadership serves good purposes, sometimes bad; but whether the end is benign or evil, great leaders are those men and women who leave their per- sonal stamp on history.

Now, the very concept of leadership implies the proposition that individuals can make a difference. This proposition has never been universally accepted. From classical times to the present day, eminent thinkers have regarded individuals as no more than the agents and pawns of larger forces, whether the gods and goddesses of the ancient world or, in the modern era, race, class, nation, the dialectic, the will of the people, the spirit of the times, history itself. Against such forces, the individual dwindles into insignificance.

So contends the thesis of historical determinism. Tolstoy's great novel *War and Peace* offers a famous statement of the case. Why, Tolstoy asked, did millions of men in the Napoleonic wars, denying their human feelings and their common sense, move back and forth across Europe slaughtering their fellows? "The war," Tolstoy answered, "was bound to happen simply because it was bound to happen." All prior history predetermined it. As for leaders, they, Tolstoy said, "are but the labels that serve to give a name to an end and, like labels, they have the least possible connection with the event." The greater the leader, "the more conspicuous the inevi- tability and the predestination of every act he commits." The leader, said Tolstoy, is "the slave of history."

Determinism takes many forms. Marxism is the determin- ism of class, Nazism the determinism of race. But the idea of men and women as the slaves of history runs athwart the deepest hu- man instincts. Rigid determinism abolishes the idea of human freedom—the assumption of free choice that underlies every move we make, every word we speak, every thought we think. It abolishes the idea of human responsibility, since it is manifestly unfair to reward or punish people for actions that are by definition beyond their control. No one can live consistently by any deterministic creed. The Marxist states prove this themselves by their extreme susceptibility to the cult of leadership.

More than that, history refutes the idea that individuals make no difference. In December 1931 a British politician crossing Park Avenue in New York City between 76th and 77th Streets around ten-thirty at night looked in the wrong direction and was knocked down by an automobile—a moment, he later recalled, of a man aghast, a world aglare: "I do not understand why I was not broken like an eggshell or·squashed like a gooseberry." Fourteen months later an American politician, sitting in an open car in Miami, Florida, was fired on by an assassin; the man beside him was hit. Those who believe that individuals make no difference to history might well ponder whether the next two decades would have been the same had Mario Contasini's car killed Winston Churchill in 1931 and Giuseppe Zangara's bullet killed Franklin Roosevelt in 1933. Suppose, in addition, that Adolf Hitler had been killed in the street fighting during the Munich *Putsch* of 1923 and that Lenin had died of typhus during the First World War. What would the 20th century be like now?

For better or for worse, individuals do make a difference. "The notion that a people can run itself and its affairs anonymously," wrote the philosopher William James, "is now well known to be the silliest of absurdities. Mankind does nothing save through initiatives on the part of inventors, great or small, and imitation by the rest of us—these are the sole factors in human progress. Individuals of genius show the way, and set the patterns, which common people then adopt and follow."

Leadership, James suggests, means leadership in thought as well as in action. In the long run, leaders in thought may well make the greater difference to the world. But, as Woodrow Wilson once said, "Those only are leaders of men, in the general eye, who lead in action. . . . It is at their hands that new thought gets its translation into the crude language of deeds." Leaders in thought often invent in solitude and obscurity, leaving to later generations the tasks of imitation. Leaders in action—the leaders portrayed in this series— have to be effective in their own time.

And they cannot be effective by themselves. They must act in response to the rhythms of their age. Their genius must be adapted, in a phrase of William James's, "to the receptivities of the moment." Leaders are useless without followers. "There goes the mob," said the French politician hearing a clamor in the streets. "I am their leader. I must follow them." Great leaders turn the inchoate emotions of the mob to purposes of their own. They seize on the opportunities of their time, the hopes, fears, frustrations, crises, potentialities.

They succeed when events have prepared the way for them, when the community is waiting to be aroused, when they can provide the clarifying and organizing ideas. Leadership ignites the circuit between the individual and the mass and thereby alters history.

It may alter history for better or for worse. Leaders have been responsible for the most extravagant follies and most monstrous crimes that have beset suffering humanity. They have also been vital in such gains as humanity has made in individual freedom, religious and racial tolerance, social justice and respect for human rights.

There is no sure way to tell in advance who is going to lead for good and who for evil. But a glance at the gallery of men and women in *World Leaders—Past and Present* suggests some useful tests.

One test is this: do leaders lead by force or by persuasion? By command or by consent? Through most of history leadership was exercised by the divine right of authority. The duty of followers was to defer and to obey. "Theirs not to reason why,/ Theirs but to do and die." On occasion, as with the so-called "enlightened despots" of the 18th century in Europe, absolutist leadership was animated by humane purposes. More often, absolutism nourished the passion for domination, land, gold and conquest and resulted in tyranny.

The great revolution of modern times has been the revolution of equality. The idea that all people should be equal in their legal condition has undermined the old structures of authority, hierarchy and deference. The revolution of equality has had two contrary effects on the nature of leadership. For equality, as Alexis de Tocqueville pointed out in his great study *Democracy in America*, might mean equality in servitude as well as equality in freedom.

"I know of only two methods of establishing equality in the political world," Tocqueville wrote. "Rights must be given to every citizen, or none at all to anyone . . . save one, who is the master of all." There was no middle ground "between the sovereignty of all and the absolute power of one man." In his astonishing prediction of 20th-century totalitarian dictatorship, Tocqueville explained how the revolution of equality could lead to the "*Führerprinzip*" and more terrible absolutism than the world had ever known.

But when rights are given to every citizen and the sovereignty of all is established, the problem of leadership takes a new form, becomes more exacting than ever before. It is easy to issue commands and enforce them by the rope and the stake, the concentration camp and the *gulag*. It is much harder to use argument and achievement to overcome opposition and win consent. The Founding Fathers of the United States understood the difficulty. They believed that history had given them the opportunity to decide, as

Alexander Hamilton wrote in the first Federalist Paper, whether men are indeed capable of basing government on "reflection and choice, or whether they are forever destined to depend . . . on accident and force."

Government by reflection and choice called for a new style of leadership and a new quality of followership. It required leaders to be responsive to popular concerns, and it required followers to be active and informed participants in the process. Democracy does not eliminate emotion from politics; sometimes it fosters demagoguery; but it is confident that, as the greatest of democratic leaders put it, you cannot fool all of the people all of the time. It measures leadership by results and retires those who overreach or falter or fail.

It is true that in the long run despots are measured by results too. But they can postpone the day of judgment, sometimes indefinitely, and in the meantime they can do infinite harm. It is also true that democracy is no guarantee of virtue and intelligence in government, for the voice of the people is not necessarily the voice of God. But democracy, by assuring the rights of opposition, offers built-in resistance to the evils inherent in absolutism. As the theologian Reinhold Niebuhr summed it up, "Man's capacity for justice makes democracy possible, but man's inclination to injustice makes democracy necessary."

A second test for leadership is the end for which power is sought. When leaders have as their goal the supremacy of a master race or the promotion of totalitarian revolution or the acquisition and exploitation of colonies or the protection of greed and privilege or the preservation of personal power, it is likely that their leadership will do little to advance the cause of humanity. When their goal is the abolition of slavery, the liberation of women, the enlargement of opportunity for the poor and powerless, the extension of equal rights to racial minorities, the defense of the freedoms of expression and opposition, it is likely that their leadership will increase the sum of human liberty and welfare.

Leaders have done great harm to the world. They have also conferred great benefits. You will find both sorts in this series. Even "good" leaders must be regarded with a certain wariness. Leaders are not demigods; they put on their trousers one leg after another just like ordinary mortals. No leader is infallible, and every leader needs to be reminded of this at regular intervals. Irreverence irritates leaders but is their salvation. Unquestioning submission corrupts leaders and demeans followers. Making a cult of a leader is always a mistake. Fortunately hero worship generates its own antidote. "Every hero," said Emerson, "becomes a bore at last."

The signal benefit the great leaders confer is to embolden the rest of us to live according to our own best selves, to be active, insistent, and resolute in affirming our own sense of things. For great leaders attest to the reality of human freedom against the supposed inevitabilities of history. And they attest to the wisdom and power that may lie within the most unlikely of us, which is why Abraham Lincoln remains the supreme example of great leadership. A great leader, said Emerson, exhibits new possibilities to all humanity. "We feed on genius. . . . Great men exist that there may be greater men."

Great leaders, in short, justify themselves by emancipating and empowering their followers. So humanity struggles to master its destiny, remembering with Alexis de Tocqueville: "It is true that around every man a fatal circle is traced beyond which he cannot pass; but within the wide verge of that circle he is powerful and free; as it is with man, so with communities."

—*New York*

1

The Path to Succession

At 4:00 A.M. on June 28, 1838, the 19-year-old Princess Victoria of England was awakened by the thunder of cannons. The Royal Artillery was firing a salute to honor her on this momentous day — the day of her coronation. She was unable to get back to sleep, since the noise from the crowd gathered outside the palace gates grew steadily louder. At 7:00 A.M. she finally gave in to her curiosity and ran to look out of her bedroom window. London's Hyde Park, normally so peaceful, was alive with holiday-makers, soldiers, and bands.

Nervous and excited, she had no appetite for the elegant breakfast she was served. However, the coronation would take almost five hours, and her own common sense argued that she should eat something. She forced herself to take a few bites.

After two seemingly endless hours had dragged by, Victoria's half-sister, Princess Feodora, came to help her dress. A white satin petticoat with gold or-namentation was fastened around Victoria's waist. She then put on a gown that was cut to show the richness of the underskirt and fell in luxuriant folds

THE BETTMANN ARCHIVE

Michael Faraday (1791–1867), English chemist. His discoveries in the fields of electricity and electro-magnetism helped power Great Britain's move into the modern age.

The coronation of Queen Victoria (1819–1901) at West-minster Abbey, June 1838. After receiving the crown from the archbishop of Canterbury and being joyously hailed by all onlookers, Victoria wrote in her diary that this was the "proudest day of my life."

behind her. Victoria then donned a crimson velvet parliamentary robe, which was lined with ermine fur and bordered with gold lace. A tasseled golden cord joined the garment at her waist. Feodora placed the finishing touch upon Victoria's head: a golden circlet set with sparkling diamonds.

At 10:00 A.M. Victoria entered the royal coach and took her place on the plush seat, which had been raised so that the petite princess would be clearly visible to her subjects. As her coach left the palace gates, a jubilant roar rose to greet her. Never before had she seen such a throng or heard such an ovation. All along her route, the crowds cheered her with unparalleled enthusiasm. She could sense their affection, their devotion — and their earnest hope that she would prove a strong leader for Britain and its empire. The coach halted in front of Westminster Abbey and the door was opened.

Upon entering the abbey, Victoria was overwhelmed by its splendor. Crimson and gold banners hung from monumental pillars, gold glittered from the altar, diamonds sparkled upon the costumes of those present. Clasping her hands and taking a deep breath, she continued down the promenade with her train-bearers in tow.

With much grace and poise she knelt before the archbishop of Canterbury and took an oath to uphold "the Protestant reformed religion as it is established by law." The archbishop anointed her with holy oil, and she withdrew to St. Edward's chapel to change for the crowning ceremony.

Victoria removed the red robe and her circlet of diamonds and donned a "singular sort of linen with lace," which was then covered by a robe of ornately embroidered gold-and-silver cloth lined with crimson silk and trimmed with gold lace.

She took her place in St. Edward's chair and received the Dalmatic robe, stiff with embroidered gold eagles, the imperial ring, the royal sceptre, and the orb of state. A ray of sunlight shone down on Victoria as the archbishop placed the crown of state on her head. Silver trumpets blared and the crowd cheered as the sovereign of Great Britain was presented to her people. Then the queen knelt before

> *Every effort must be made to keep the education of the daughter completely in the hands of her mother and to prevent all interference. Nothing and no one should be able to tear the daughter away from her.*
> —PRINCE CHARLES OF LENINGEN
> Victoria's half-brother,
> describing the aims of the
> Kensington System

the archbishop and humbly received the Sacrament. When Victoria rose, the abbey rang with Handel's *Hallelujah Chorus*.

That evening, Victoria turned to her journal despite her weariness. There she recorded the events of the day, and concluded that she would "remember this as the proudest day of my life."

Queen Victoria had good reason to be proud on that day, and the many that followed. Her reign was to help usher in a period of enormous change, both for Great Britain and for the world.

However, this grand destiny was not readily apparent when Victoria was born in 1819. At that

An illustration by French painter Paul-Gustave Doré (1832—83) shows the crowded living conditions in mid-19th-century London. Though rapid industrialization in England at the time brought prosperity to some people, it meant poverty for many others. Queen Victoria and Prince Albert (1819—61) made the plight of the poor one of their main concerns.

time, the throne of Great Britain was the greatest prize in Europe. The wealthy empire it governed extended over Africa, Asia, and the Americas. But the empire's stability depended upon a smooth succession of leadership. The ailing George III was king of Great Britain and prince of Hanover, a small state in Germany. He had produced fifteen children, of whom seven sons and five daughters survived. The eldest son, George, had been appointed prince regent, which meant that he governed the empire for George III, who was suffering from a chronic disease that was making him insane.

The prince regent had fathered a charming daughter, Princess Charlotte, who was, after her father, next in line to the throne. Lively and attractive, she married Prince Leopold of Saxe-Coburg, Germany, at the age of 18. She was popular throughout England and there was great rejoicing at her wedding.

Eighteen months after her marriage, Princess Charlotte died in childbirth on November 6, 1817. As England mourned her loss, the political elite realized that her death had created a serious problem.

All of King George III's seven sons were well into middle age, and none had produced any legitimate children. In the year following Charlotte's death, three of George III's sons married, intending to provide heirs for the succession.

One of these three sons, Edward, the duke of Kent, married Princess Victoria of Saxe-Coburg, a widow and the mother of two children, Charles and Feodora.

The family moved to Germany, and soon thereafter, the duchess was discovered to be with child. Fearing that the legitimacy of the infant's claim to the throne would be harmed if the child was born outside England, the duke began to make plans for their return.

However, the duke was not popular with his royal relatives, and they did not encourage his return. Since he was invariably short of funds and deeply in debt, it was difficult for him to undertake the expense of such a journey himself. It was not until the duchess was in her eighth month that the royal party was ready to make the journey to England.

King George III made a suite of rooms available to them in the luxurious Kensington Palace. These arrangements did not indicate any return to royal favor, however. Rather, the king had been put in a position where royal protocol demanded that he provide suitable lodgings.

The duchess of Kent gave birth to a baby girl at 4:15 A.M. on May 24, 1819. That the child was female was not a cause for disappointment: as the infant's German grandmother pointed out, "The English like Queens."

As if to emphasize this almost prophetic comment, a small group of political notables were waiting in the next room. This group included the duke of Wellington, who had commanded the forces that defeated Napoleon at Waterloo, as well as the archbishop of Canterbury, the head of the Church of England. Also in attendance were the bishop of London and members of the Privy Council, the hand-picked advisers of the king, all of whom breathed sighs of relief at the birth of a legitimate successor.

Despite this glad event, the duke and his family were still unpopular with their relatives. The duke of Kent had never enjoyed the affection of his parents, and his brother, the prince regent, all but hated him. The duchess was also held in low esteem, since she had terrible difficulty learning English and was felt to be *too* German. This prejudice may seem peculiar, given the royal family's many ties to Germany. However, the English of that period frequently had a bias against foreigners, their customs, and their languages. The members of the royal family expressed their strong desire that the duchess "feel free" to return to her own country — taking her family with her. The duke, though, was determined not to give in. He clung to his native land in order to strengthen his child's claim to the throne.

Princess Victoria's first official appearance was at her christening, where family difficulties arose, foreshadowing the trying years ahead. In accordance with tradition, her father submitted a list of possible names for the princess to the prince regent.

In every letter I shall write to you, I mean to repeat to you, as a fundamental rule, to be courageous, firm and honest, as you have been till now.
—KING LEOPOLD I OF BELGIUM
Victoria's uncle, upon learning of her succession

Portrait of King George III (1738–1820) by A. Ramsay. George III ruled England during the American War of Independence, after which his influence began to wane. His fourth son, Edward, duke of Kent (1767–1820), was Victoria's father.

THE BETTMANN ARCHIVE

The duke had planned to name her "Victoire Georgina Alexandrina Charlotte Augusta." The prince regent, furious at the prospect of his younger brother producing the heir to the throne, refused to allow the child any of the traditional names of the English royal family. He would only allow Alexandrina, which was given to honor her godfather, Tsar Alexander of Russia. When pressed by the duke of Kent, the prince regent made one small concession: "Give her the mother's name also then, but it cannot precede that of the emperor of Russia." The infant was christened Alexandrina Victoria. She was called Victoria in official circles, while her pet name as a child was Drina, the diminutive form of Alexandrina.

Although important members of the royal family treated the little princess as an intruder, Victoria became a high-spirited child. Her father wrote of her, "The little one is rather a pocket of Hercules than a pocket of Venus."

When Victoria was eight months old, her father was taken ill with a severe cold. His condition worsened and was aggravated by the ineptitude of his doctors. He died on January 23, 1820, after prolonged suffering.

His death marked the beginning of a different sort of life for Victoria and her family, as they became the victims of political intriguers and the animosity of the prince regent. Their vulnerability to these forces was increased when, only six days after the death of the duke of Kent, his father King George III died. After nine years as prince regent, George IV ascended the throne.

The duke of Kent had left his wife nothing but debts. He had died while they were staying by the sea at Sidmouth, and his widow and daughter did not even have the money for their return journey to London.

With no means of support, and the animosity of the English court to contend with, they were fortunate to have one protector close at hand. The duchess's brother, Prince Leopold of Saxe-Coburg, had remained in England after the death of his beloved wife, Princess Charlotte. He took his sister and young niece under his protection.

George IV, the new king, begrudgingly allowed his brother's family to return to Kensington Palace. However, it was Prince Leopold who supported them and paid for Victoria's education. Fully aware of the

Portrait of Victoria shortly after she became queen of England in 1837. For most of her youth Victoria was isolated from society and the royal family. This "Kensington system" of raising her was aimed at purifying the throne and dissociating her from the moral outrages of her relatives.

Princess Victoria of Saxe-Coburg-Gotha, the duchess of Kent (1786–1861). An overly protective, dominating mother, she slept in the same room as her daughter every night until the day the young heiress ascended the throne.

difficulties of his sister's life, he nonetheless convinced her that she and her daughter must remain in England. Victoria had to grow up as an English child, lest her claim to the throne be jeopardized.

Prince Leopold was not the only person whom the duchess could lean on in time of adversity. However, he was the only one she could trust. The other "ally" was Captain John Conroy, a former member of the late duke's personal staff. Conroy was a man of ability and great charm, but he was also unscrupulous and ambitious.

Conroy perceived that the duchess's lonely and desperate situation, combined with the possible destiny of her daughter, afforded him a perfect opportunity for advancement. He hoped that by becoming the family's most trusted friend, he would gain a hold over the princess.

The duchess did, in fact, become completely dependent upon Captain Conroy, and together they devised a system for bringing up and educating Victoria. The system, which became known as the "Kensington System," was designed to prevent anyone other than the duchess and captain themselves from gaining influence over the little princess.

The duke of Kent. Though the duke was not popular with his royal relations — owing to his perpetual indebtedness — he alone among George III's seven sons had sired a legitimate heir to the throne. He died just eight months after Victoria's birth.

Everyone who came into contact with her was under constant scrutiny, to the point that she was never allowed to have a visitor without a third person acting as overseer.

Although this intense chaperoning denied Victoria the benefits of living in society, there was a sound political reason for isolating the princess. This was the only way to disassociate her from the stories of debauchery and licentiousness that had ruined the reputation of her father's family. When the time came to present Victoria as heir to the throne, she was to be of irreproachable character, unconnected to the moral outrages of her relatives. Her mother's family, the Coburgs, were also of dubious repute, but since these relatives were further away, discouraging their contact was simple.

The Kensington System permitted only one person to dominate the princess: her mother. Victoria was encouraged to be completely dependent upon her; she even slept in her mother's room every night.

Eventually Conroy and the duchess worked out a plan for introducing the princess to the outside world. The captain urged that Victoria be presented in such a way that the duchess's position as mother and responsible guardian would receive the most emphasis. In this way, were George IV to die before Victoria had reached 18 (the minimum age at which one could ascend the throne), the duchess would be named as Victoria's regent until she came of age. Conroy hoped that his influence over the duchess would then make him Victoria's unofficial regent. The plan was more simple than subtle, but it still held great promise for Conroy. That promise grew ever brighter as, one by one, the remaining heirs who stood between Victoria and the throne were removed, either by death, debarment, or infirmity.

While Conroy and the duchess were carefully cul-

Princess Victoria at the age of four. Legend has it that the child heiress, upon being told that she would someday be queen of England, replied, "I will be good."

tivating their chances to rise in rank and power, Victoria was enduring the consequences of the Kensington System, a sad fate for a lively little girl.

In her early years, Victoria had enjoyed the companionship of her half-sister, Princess Feodora. Even though there was a twelve-year difference in their ages, the two girls were devoted companions. Conroy and the duchess, however, regarded even this intimacy with mistrust, and Conroy coolly engineered a marriage for Feodora in order to remove her from the household.

Princess Feodora's departure from the world of Kensington Palace indirectly caused an important person to enter Victoria's life. This person was Baroness Louise Lehzen, who had previously been engaged as Feodora's governess. She had come, with strong recommendations, from Germany, and was both intelligent and attractive. The baroness was a woman of strong character, absolutely dedicated to her charges. Victoria was placed under the baroness's care when she was five years old and remained her pupil until she was eighteen.

Conroy decided to employ Baroness Lehzen primarily because she was German, and therefore was less likely to have dangerous political connections. He reasoned that an English governess might have powerful friends who would try to influence Victoria.

Victoria was not an easy responsibility; she was obstinate and displayed a quick temper. But Baroness Lehzen loved the young princess, and patiently helped her to overcome her more tempestuous outbursts. Obstinacy, however, was a lifelong trait of Victoria's, one which she occasionally recognized but never fully suppressed.

Baroness Lehzen was Victoria's main instructor, but other teachers came in for special studies. The little princess had a regular, somewhat rigid, schedule, which included lessons in English, French, German, religion, drawing, dancing, and singing. Later, Latin was added to the curriculum, and later still, Victoria studied Sir William Blackstone's important political analysis, *Commentaries on English Laws.*

> *But without Lehzen's strength, Lehzen's support, Lehzen's not unimportant influence in high places, it is doubtful if Princess Victoria would have survived the 'Kensington System.'*
> —CECIL WOODHAM-SMITH
> British historian

In 1826, when Victoria was seven years old, King George IV relented a little towards his deceased brother's family, perhaps because of the irresistible charm of Princess Feodora. The duchess received an invitation to the royal lodge at Windsor, and Victoria had the privilege of being lifted into the royal carriage. She was treated kindly and indulgently by the king, who was charmed by her manners and cleverness. She, in turn, enjoyed the grandeur of the event immensely. Thus, the great rift between her and her royal relatives closed somewhat — a trench now, rather than a canyon.

When Victoria was 11, it was decided that she should be examined on the progress of her studies, an occasion that Conroy hoped would win recognition for the duchess's success in grooming and educating a royal princess. The bishops of London and Lincoln were invited to attend, and were duly impressed by the princess's progress. They also inquired whether Victoria had yet been made aware of her probable future. She had not.

Baroness Lehzen recorded what happened when young Victoria was told that she might be queen. According to the governess, when she gave Victoria the family tree showing the line of succession, Victoria said, "I see I am nearer to the throne than I thought." Then she made her famous vow, "I will be good."

In June 1830 George IV died, and his brother the duke of Clarence became King William IV.

In a mounting series of disagreements stemming from mutual lack of understanding the new king and the duchess of Kent reopened the old rift. The key point of friction was that the new king wished the princess, now heiress apparent, to take part in court functions. To Captain Conroy and the duchess, this presented an obvious danger; the princess would begin to enter into a life independent of her mother and the Kensington System. Conroy and the duchess thus saw their plans crumbling and took steps to prevent Victoria's attendance at court. The duchess, without blatantly refusing to allow the princess to come to court, managed to put obstacles in the way. The king was disappointed — and an-

Every effort must be made to keep the education of the daughter completely in the hands of her mother and to prevent all interference. Nothing and no one should be able to tear the daughter away from her.
—PRINCE CHARLES OF LEININGEN
Victoria's half-brother, describing the aims of the Kensington System

Windsor Castle has been the principal residence of the British royal family since the 11th century.

noyed — that he didn't see his niece at court more often.

Conroy and the duchess began to organize a series of tours around Britain to allow the princess to gain some familiarity with the country she was to rule. On these journeys, their entourage visited great country houses so that she might meet some of her most powerful future subjects. At each town she visited, speeches were given, guns were fired in salute, bands played, and the streets were decorated with flags and flowers. The fact that these celebrations were a great success further irritated the king. He felt that the duchess was flaunting the position she and her daughter would inherit at his death. The journeys were not particularly pleasing to Victoria either, who found that they drained her energy.

Since it has pleased Providence to place me in this station, I shall do my utmost to fulfill my duty towards my country; I am very young, and perhaps in many, though not all things, inexperienced, but I am sure, that very few have more real good will and more real desire to do what is fit and right than I have.

—QUEEN VICTORIA
writing in her diary on
June 20, 1837, upon
learning of her succession

Victoria's position was becoming increasingly trying and lonely. At home, there were constant intrigues and bickerings, and she was aware that efforts were being made to dismiss Baroness Lehzen, who had become, in Conroy's opinion, too intimate with the princess. In addition, Victoria had to try to keep from becoming involved in unending quarrels with her uncle, the king. Victoria's only refuges were her lessons and her governess, who guided and supported her, with discretion and tact, throughout these troubled times. It was a tedious life for a young girl. Yet, in the midst of it all, she remained affectionate, sincere, and fully appreciative of the few pleasures that brightened her often dull existence.

After her seventeenth birthday, the question of Victoria's marriage received serious consideration. Victoria's Uncle Leopold arranged a visit by the two

Edinburgh Castle, which dates from the 11th century, dominates the Scottish capital. Victoria and Albert spent a good deal of their leisure time in Scotland.

princes of Saxe-Coburg-Gotha, Ernest and Albert. Albert, the second born, had always been the favorite. In Victoria's opinion, Albert was the more handsome of the two, and she liked him very much on this first visit. All the same, she was disappointed that he did not much enjoy dancing, preferring to go to bed early.

On Victoria's eighteenth birthday all Conroy's hopes of a regency were dashed. Victoria had attained the age of majority and, if placed on the throne, could rule for herself. Conroy began a campaign, aided by the duchess, to force from Victoria a written promise that she would appoint him as her private secretary. The princess, although weak with typhoid at the time, refused.

As the health of the 72-year-old king deteriorated, Conroy grew increasingly desperate, trying to apply pressure in every possible way. The only rewards he

Buckingham Palace, the London residence of the British monarchy.

One of the heiress's future subjects pays his respects. As Victoria approached the age of 18 — at which time she would legally assume the throne — she was gradually introduced to the people and the country she was to rule.

received for his troubles were Victoria's steady refusals and her lasting dislike.

King William IV's condition worsened rapidly. On June 18, 1837, the princess wrote in her diary, "The poor King, they say, can live but a few hours now." On the evening of June 19, William's last reserves of strength began to fail.

Victoria recorded the events of the following day in her journal: "I was awoke at 6 o'clock by Mamma who told me that the archbishop of Canterbury and Lord Conyngham were here and wished to see me. I got out of bed and went into my sitting room (only in my dressing gown) and *alone*, and saw them. Lord Conyngham (the lord chamberlain) then acquainted me that my poor uncle, the king, was no more, and had expired at 12 minutes past 2 this morning and consequently that *I* am *Queen*."

Numb. 19795.

2411

The London Gazette
EXTRAORDINARY.

Published by Authority.

SATURDAY, NOVEMBER 23, 1839.

HER Majesty being this day present in Council, was pleased to make the following Declaration, viz.

I HAVE caused you to be summoned at the present time, in order that I may acquaint you with my resolution in a matter which deeply concerns the welfare of My people, and the happiness of my future life.

It is My intention to ally Myself in Marriage with the Prince Albert of Saxe Cobourg and Gotha. Deeply impressed with the solemnity of the engagement which I am about to contract, I have not come to this decision without mature consideration, nor without feeling a strong assurance that, with the blessing of Almighty God, it will at once secure my domestic felicity and serve the interests of my country.

I have thought fit to make this resolution known to you at the earliest period, in order that you may be fully apprised of a matter so highly important to Me and to My kingdom, and which I persuade Myself will be most acceptable to all My loving subjects.

Whereupon all the Privy Councillors present, made it their humble request to Her Majesty, that Her Majesty's Most Gracious Declaration to them might be made public; which Her Majesty was pleased to order accordingly.

C. C. Greville.

2

The Young Queen

Her bearing at her first Council filled the whole gathering with astonishment and admiration.
—LYTTON STRACHEY
British historian

As Victoria prepared to begin her reign, the effect of the Kensington System's isolation became evident; she was almost unknown to her subjects — including some of the most powerful political figures in the realm.

On the first day of her reign, her special advisers (known as the Privy Council) assembled at 11:30 A.M. They knew little about the queen except that she was young and reputed to be fairly astute.

Victoria entered alone, bowed to the gathered notables, took her seat at the head of the long table, and read her statement in a voice both clear and composed. There was no hint of the nervousness she felt as she completed this task or received their oaths of loyalty. With a cordial farewell, she withdrew, her exit as poised and graceful as her entrance. After a stunned moment, the council broke into relieved conversation; their opinion of her was unanimously positive. Some praised her composure and confidence, others her seriousness and evident competence. But if there was one factor that was deemed the most positive, it was simply that she was intent on becoming a responsible sovereign.

An extract from *The London Gazette* announcing Queen Victoria's plans to marry Prince Albert of Saxe-Coburg-Gotha. To the surprise of almost everyone — the young couple included — the two fell in love almost immediately and went on to forge one of the most successful royal marriages in history.

THE BETTMANN ARCHIVE

THE BETTMANN ARCHIVE

Lord Melbourne (1779–1848), Queen Victoria's first prime minister. An intelligent, handsome aristocrat, Melbourne became something of a father figure to the young sovereign, teaching her not only about the responsibilities of state and ceremony, but also about the peculiarities of human nature — to which Victoria had rarely been exposed.

After a long series of disreputable monarchs, it seemed that in Victoria, the British throne at last had an occupant who would restore it to its previous position of respect and honor.

Victoria immediately began to restructure those aspects of her life that did not befit her new role as queen. She moved her bed out of her mother's room, and her first night as queen was also the first night she slept alone. This newfound sense of independence — facing the Privy Council by herself, and having the privacy of a personal chamber — was exhilarating for Victoria. Her journal entry on that first day betrays this excitement; several times she makes special mention of the fact that she did something "alone."

But the new queen required more than independence; she needed a counselor since the intricacies of her position and British politics were areas in which she lacked extensive education. Her need for such a mentor was quickly satisfied.

Just before the young queen had met the Privy Council, she was introduced to her prime minister, Lord Melbourne. Victoria formally assured him that she intended to retain him at his post, and he responded by kissing her hand — the ceremonial gesture by which prime ministers swear loyalty to Crown and country. Although Victoria remained calm upon meeting Melbourne, her journal attests to the fact that she was immediately impressed by him. At 58, Melbourne was not only at the height of his career, but still possessed good looks, which the young queen did not fail to notice. As their acquaintance grew into friendship, she also noted that he was a gifted conversationalist, was well read, and had a unique wit. Also of great importance to Victoria was that Melbourne was an aristocrat, a person of standing nearly equal to her own, with whom she felt comfortable and relaxed.

Melbourne quickly became aware that he had an impressionable young girl to educate and counsel, a young girl who had inherited the awesome responsibilities of the English throne. On a practical level, she was fortunate to have so qualified a teacher, and he so talented a pupil, but beyond this

It has long been my intention to retain your Lordship and the rest of the present ministry at the head of affairs.
—QUEEN VICTORIA
speaking to the incumbent
prime minister, Lord
Melbourne, after
becoming queen

they were both simply happy for the other's companionship. Their attachment grew rapidly. Melbourne thought of the young queen as almost a daughter; Victoria thought her beloved "Lord M." kind, witty, intelligent, shrewd, and charming.

The prime minister unofficially assumed the duties of Victoria's teacher and private secretary. He instructed her on the British constitution, the workings of the government, and the significance of various policies. He helped her with a great deal of the overwhelming paperwork with which she, as queen, had to contend. But equally important, it was Lord Melbourne who helped her emerge from the isolation of Kensington Palace into the bright world of human society.

One result of Victoria's independence was an increasing distance from her mother. Although they both took up residence at Buckingham Palace in July 1838, and Victoria's public behavior towards her mother was always beyond reproach, the young queen did not permit any actual intimacy between them. The duchess of Kent was given a separate apartment and was informed that she would now have to make an appointment if she wanted to see her daughter.

The many new experiences and challenges Victoria encountered were made more enjoyable by the constant companionship of Lord Melbourne. She

Queen Victoria thanking a conductor after an orchestral performance. Victoria's first months as queen were marked by many public festivities and entertainments, as she reveled in her independence and popularity.

Robert Peel (1788–1850), the Tory who replaced Melbourne as prime minister in 1841. Though Peel had two years earlier offended Victoria during the "bedchamber crisis," his effectiveness as a statesman, leader, and reformer later won her admiration.

opened Parliament, held official parties, and received guests and supplicants. It seemed as if everyone wished to meet her, and for those who managed to, they were invariably charmed by her dignity, courtesy, and kindness. She reveled in her popularity and success.

Aside from her official duties her days were often spent horseback riding, accompanied by Lord Melbourne, through Windsor Great Park. The evenings were filled with amusement and entertainment. Lord Melbourne abandoned other interests and more sophisticated company to sit with her over puzzles or chess. But above all, young Victoria loved to dance, and there were balls aplenty for her to attend. She enjoyed popular dances such as the mazurka and quadrille, but because she felt it improper for a subject's arm to hold her waist, she would not waltz.

The only shadow cast on this happiness was that of Captain Conroy, who continued his role as her mother's close ally. To Victoria's annoyance, the duchess of Kent steadfastly refused to change this.

Conroy finally declared himself ready to retire, but his demands for a large pension and a peerage (a title of nobility, such as duke or earl) were extravagant. Lord Melbourne eventually convinced Conroy to accept a more modest pension and the first available Irish peerage.

But Victoria's continuing resentment of her mother was to bear ugly and unexpected consequences. Early in 1839 one of the duchess's ladies-in-waiting, the unmarried Lady Flora Hastings, was observed to have an enlarged stomach. Not only did Victoria suspect her of being pregnant, she also believed that Lady Hastings was a spy for Captain Conroy. Victoria also disliked the lady-in-waiting for her membership in one of the most powerful Tory families in England, because the Tories were the bitter political opponents of Victoria's beloved Whig, Lord M. Supported by Baroness Lehzen, Victoria ostracized the unfortunate Lady Hastings.

Later when a medical examination suggested that Lady Hastings was neither pregnant nor sexually experienced, Victoria was slow to relent. Her suspicion and obstinacy persisted even when it became evident that Lady Hasting's condition was caused by grave illness. A public outcry arose against her unjustified ostracism. In the end, the young queen attempted to make amends, but it was too late. Lady Hastings died on July 5, and her postmortem examination showed that her abdominal swelling and her death had been caused by a tumor on the liver. Victoria's popularity plummeted. Lady Hastings had died a martyr, and Victoria was perceived as the villain of the whole tragic affair. There were hisses in the royal enclosure when she attended the horse races at Ascot, and booing greeted her carriage when it appeared in the streets.

Even before this disaster had passed, a new worry arose. Lord Melbourne's Whig party was growing steadily weaker in Parliament, such that it was becoming evident that Melbourne might soon have to resign as prime minister.

The English system of government maintains that the prime minister holds his office only as long as his party holds the most seats in the House of

The new queen was almost entirely unknown to her subjects. In her public appearances her mother had almost invariably dominated the scene. Her private life had been that of a novice in a convent; hardly a human being from the outside world had even spoken to her; and no human being at all except for her mother and the Baroness Lehzen had ever been alone with her in a room.
—LYTTON STRACHEY
British historian

Commons (the representative branch of government). If the prime minister loses this advantage, he is expected to offer his resignation to the reigning monarch. The sovereign then appoints a new prime minister — usually from the new "majority" party.

The Whig party (which was later absorbed into the Liberal party) was primarily composed of aristocrats, who in recent years had struck a temporary alliance with the powerful Dissenters (Protestants who were not members of the Church of England, also known as the Anglican church) in order to bring about the Reform Act of 1832. This act, which further extended voting privileges only to middle-class men, brought about further restrictions on the powers of England's monarch.

Opposing the Whigs were the Tories, a political party largely comprised of wealthy landowners and influential Anglican churchmen.

The party of conservatism, the Tories defended the rigid class divisions that characterized Victorian England. Staunch believers in society as it was, the Tories believed that reform should always be gradual; radical change was not to be tolerated. To them, society naturally consisted of rich and poor. Government should be efficient and maintain order, but not interfere with these classes. Although these were the party's principles, the Tories would institute several key reforms between 1822 and 1827. By 1830, they became known as the Conservative party, and had grown so unified that they proved stronger than the Whigs.

In May 1839 Melbourne gave in to the inevitable, and handed Victoria his resignation. The young queen was devastated, as her journal entry shows: "All, all my happiness gone! That happy peaceful life destroyed, and dearest kind Lord Melbourne no more my minister." But she soon learned that she was losing more than a minister; she would virtually lose him as a friend. Melbourne was too politically powerful to continue visiting her socially; the Tories would never stand for it, fearing that he would sway her opinion against them. Melbourne, realizing the sensitivity of the situation, suggested that Victoria send for the duke of Wellington to advise her regarding the formation of a new government. The finality of the situation began to grow painfully clear to the young queen; she was to lose her friend, mentor, tutor, and companion all in one stroke. Her old feelings of loneliness began to return.

The duke of Wellington's advice only made her feel worse: he suggested that she ask Sir Robert Peel, a prominent Tory, to form the new government. Although she found Peel abrasive, Victoria understood her role as a constitutional monarch very well. She knew she could not appoint a minister and expect the House of Commons to go along with her simply because she was queen. That sort of insistence would only pave the way for further restrictions on her monarchical powers. Victoria resigned herself to the situation, took Wellington's advice, and sent for Peel.

However, as is often the case in politics, it was not a great issue that caused difficulty between them, but a seemingly insignificant one. Peel was concerned that all of Victoria's ladies of the bedchamber were Whigs, and requested that she dismiss several and replace them with Tory ladies. The indignant young queen flatly refused to make any alterations in the royal household. When this first meeting ended it was clear that a major dispute was brewing, a dispute that came to be known as the "Bedchamber Crisis."

Lord Melbourne realized that Victoria was shaken by the change of ministry, being young and unaccustomed to the rigors of politics. Consequently, he thought it best that she keep the familiar and friendly members of her household around her. Melbourne advised the young queen to explain this to Peel, and to remind him that his request was without precedent. Victoria agreed to this plan and called for a second meeting with Peel.

But Victoria was not able to detach her political actions from her personal feelings. She simply did not like Peel, whom she found to be a "cold, odd man," infinitely inferior to the handsome and congenial Melbourne.

Their second meeting was very strained. When Peel reiterated his request that certain ladies be

They wish to treat me like a girl, but I will show them that I am Queen of England.

—QUEEN VICTORIA
to Lord Melbourne
concerning the
Bedchamber Question,
May 1855

dismissed, Victoria's indignation returned — this time bordering on outrage. She argued that the ladies' appointments were her personal affair, and that she never discussed politics with them. Peel countered by pointing out that some of her ladies were married to his most powerful political opponents.

The meeting ended in a complete stalemate. Despite the intervention of the duke of Wellington, perhaps the most influential man in the country, Victoria remained firm in her position. In the end, Peel rejected the position of prime minister, convinced that he could not accept it under such circumstances.

Lord Melbourne quickly called his cabinet together and put the problem before its members. He explained that the queen was young, alone in her position, and was shocked and insulted at having a minister attempt to dictate her household arrangement. He then read two letters from the distraught young queen, thus winning the cabinet's sympathy. They decided that she should not have to dismiss any of her ladies. Lord Melbourne was immediately reinstated as prime minister, even though the Whigs were still a minority in Parliament.

The young queen had displayed a will of iron. While it was only proper that the cabinet showed sympathy for Victoria's difficult position, they also showed considerable respect for her strength and tenacity. The press was quick to pick up on this, expressing outrage at the fact that the "whims" of a young girl could determine the ministry of the country.

All in all, 1839 had been a sobering year for Victoria. She had learned that being a queen involved at least as much controversy and compromise as it did magnificence and splendor. She had seen her popularity plummet, and her policies and opinions subjected to bitter attack.

These pressures contributed to the further erosion of Victoria's relationship with the duchess of Kent. The young queen complained about her mother constantly, finding her presence to be an unending source of difficulty and irritation. However, by the standards of the day, the only way that the duchess could be established in a completely separate household was if Victoria were to marry.

The young queen had not given the idea of marriage much thought, and in fact, was not very enthusiastic about the subject. She greatly enjoyed her newfound independence and feared that marriage would mean the end of such freedom.

However, other factors forced her to consider her marital possibilities. Chief among these factors was that, should she die without children, the remaining line of succession was highly undesirable. First in line was her uncle, the duke of Cambridge, an unpopular figure who some suspected would return the throne to its previous state of disrepute. After him, there was his blind son — and that was where

The British Houses of Parliament and the famous "Big Ben" clock tower are both located in London along the River Thames.

the line ended. Victoria could sense that England wished to see her married and the mother of suitable heirs to the throne.

Her Uncle Leopold had long suggested that she marry her cousin, Prince Albert of Saxe-Coburg-Gotha. The prince came from the house of Coburg in the German state of Saxony. Since it was considered virtually taboo to marry subjects, members of royal houses were obligated to marry only members of other royal houses. Following the Napoleonic Wars, Germany was partitioned in 1815 by the treaty of Vienna into 38 principalities; the number of marriageable young nobles was greatly increased. King Leopold of Belgium, who had been the prince of Saxony, with his aide, Baron Stockmar, groomed the second son of his eldest brother specifically to marry Princess Victoria. Baron Stockmar went on, along with Baroness Lehzen, to become a trusted adviser in matters of the queen's household.

Melbourne expressed some doubt over this; he knew his countrymen and doubted that a foreign prince would be popular with them. But Victoria responded to Melbourne's reservations with an unusual degree of independence. She felt that in the matter of marriage, her own preference was the most important consideration. She had already decided that she would not marry one of her subjects, so she and Melbourne sat down to study the list of eligible princes. At the end of their deliberations, Victoria was still undecided regarding marriage. Albert was scheduled to visit England in October, and she felt that the matter could wait until then.

Since his last visit to London in 1836, Albert had traveled widely in Europe, acquiring a fine education and broad perspective that he hoped would prepare him for a role in governmental leadership. The subtleties of court life had not been ignored either; serious-minded Albert had taken dancing lessons in order to please the fun-loving Victoria. He wrote to his tutor, "I am to go into society, learn the ways of the world and vitiate my culture with fashionable accomplishments, that last of which would appear to be an extraordinary good testimonial in Victoria's eyes." But Albert was certainly not blinded by love;

he had a realistic outlook on what life with Victoria might be like, writing, "Victoria is said to be incredibly stubborn, and her extreme obstinacy to be constantly at war with her good nature . . . she delights in Court ceremonies, etiquette and trivial formalities . . . she is said not to take the slightest pleasure in nature and to enjoy sitting up at night and sleeping late into the day."

It certainly did not promise to be a love match. The prospect of Albert's October visit began to make Victoria nervous, and she wrote what was almost a letter of warning to her Uncle Leopold. She stressed that she would not enter into any marriage that had been arranged by her family, and that she had never made any promises concerning Albert.

Promises proved to be unnecessary. In the two years since their last meeting, Albert had matured into an extremely handsome young man. Victoria, susceptible as she was to charm and good looks, fell in love almost immediately. Her journal is eloquent testimony to her feelings for Albert, "Such beautiful eyes, an exquisite nose, and such a pretty mouth with delicate moustachios and very slight whiskers: a beautiful figure, broad in the shoulders and a fine waist; my heart is quite going." Although this praise might seem excessive, it nonetheless offers excellent insight into Victoria's mind. She was a woman of remarkably strong and swift emotions, living in a world filled with feelings, people, and events that were all larger than life.

Albert was charmed by Victoria's affectionate and compassionate nature. The one thing that neither one of them had expected had occurred: they had fallen in love.

But as a penniless German prince, protocol forbade Albert to propose to the queen of England. It was up to Victoria to make the proposal.

Albert had been in England for less than a week when Victoria earnestly offered him "her hand and her heart." "The joyous openness of manner in which she told me this," wrote the prince to his grandmother, "quite enchanted me, and I was quite carried away by it."

Before their wedding could take place Albert had

There is something which shocks one's sense of fitness and propriety in the spectacle of this mere baby of a Queen setting herself in opposition to this great man [the duke of Wellington].
—CHARLES GREVILLE
British diarist and clerk to the privy council

to return to his native Coburg in order to conclude his business there. In many ways, this was a painful visit for the young prince. His marriage to Victoria meant a final parting from his beloved homeland, its people, and his family. In their place, he had to be prepared to live most of his life in urban England, forever regarded as a foreigner. He did not enjoy his adopted nation's climate, nor its cuisine, and his position as prince consort to a queen would require constant flexibility and patience.

It was in this difficult premarital period that Albert quickly proved that he had a large capacity for fairness and patience, qualities that would later earn him the affectionate nickname "Albert the Good." This goodness was immediately put to the test by the imperious manner in which Victoria made arrangements for him during his absence from London. For instance, she insisted on appointing his private secretary herself. Albert justifiably protested that he alone should make the selection. Victoria disagreed, feeling she had the superior judgment in the matter, and confirmed the appointment she had already made. Parliament was also haggling over the allowance Albert was to be awarded, finally settling on a sum well below that which had been expected originally. Understandably, Albert had doubts about his welcome in England. Despite these feelings, his letters to Victoria continued to be remarkable for their loving tone.

Although Victoria thought herself lucky to have such a happy marriage, her country was to benefit at least as much. From the first day of their marriage until the end of his life, Albert dedicated all of his energies to his adopted country. His discretion, advice, and above all, his intelligence, made him invaluable to both the queen and her realm.

Victoria and Albert were married on February 10, 1840, in the Chapel Royal at St. James's Palace. Victoria wore a white satin gown, a diamond necklace and earrings, and a magnificent sapphire brooch that Albert had given her. Twelve bridesmaids, all in white, carried her train.

The couple decided to go away for a few days following the wedding. Albert had desired a longer

Her chief fault (in little things and great) seems to be impatience; in Sea phrase, she always wants to go ahead; she can't bear contradiction nor to be thwarted.
—ADOLPHUS FITZCLARENCE
British gentleman

honeymoon, so that they could have an opportunity to spend a certain period of time alone together as they began their marriage. But Victoria, ever conscious of her duties, insisted that their holiday be brief. Her reply was firm, "My dear Albert, you have not at all understood the matter. You forget, my dearest love, that I am the sovereign, and that business cannot stop and wait. . . ."

As the newlyweds prepared to depart for Windsor on their holiday, Lord Melbourne came to say farewell and give Victoria his blessing. It was a more significant farewell than she realized at the time, for the lord's role as counselor and teacher was soon transferred completely to Albert.

Their carriage encountered an almost unbroken crowd of cheering well-wishers along their route to Windsor Castle. The queen, small and graceful, and the tall, handsome prince at her side filled with hope the hearts of those who saw them.

Thus began one of the happiest — and most politically successful — royal marriages in history.

Prince Albert (doffing his top hat) and Queen Victoria ride in the royal carriage on the way to Windsor Castle following their wedding in February 1840. Well-wishers and spectators thronged most of the 22-mile route.

At the opening of Parliament, 1846, Queen Victoria delivers a speech as Prince Albert looks on. Victoria ruled at a time of steadily increasing challenges to monarchies throughout Europe, as "common" people fought for more legislative and administrative power.

3

Royal Consort

Victoria found her marriage to Albert to be the source of her greatest joy; her fears of lost freedom were totally forgotten. But as is true with all couples, the first months were filled with the recurrent challenge of adjusting and adapting to one another. In many ways, Victoria and Albert were very different people.

Victoria was expressive in the extreme, showing none of the repressed qualities long associated with the "Victorian era." She was frank in expressing her feelings to Albert, and adored him fervently. The queen still loved dancing, the theater, games, and a relaxed home life where bedtimes and risings tended to be late.

Albert was a reserved man who possessed conservative tastes in all things. He was serious, hardworking, studious, and fond of the still beauty of the countryside and the challenge of high-minded discussions with philosophers and artists. The queen frequently reacted to such intellectual gatherings with discomfort, often feeling herself at a disadvantage.

However, there were many pursuits that they both

SNARK/ART RESOURCE

Friedrich Engels (1820–95), the German economist and socialist. Engels collaborated with Karl Marx (1818–83) to formulate the *Communist Manifesto*; among his other works was a harsh critique of capitalism entitled *The Condition of the Working Class in England*.

German composer Felix Mendelssohn (1809–47) — one of Prince Albert's favorites — plays for the royal couple in the 1840s. Mendelssohn made several triumphant trips to England during his short but illustrious career.

enjoyed and that served to bring them closer together. Riding, music, and dancing proved to be favorite royal pastimes. In fact, Albert, who originally had not cared for dancing, now proved himself to be uncommonly graceful and skilled at it. Perhaps most importantly, Albert expanded Victoria's limited circle of friends by introducing her to the artists and thinkers he held in high esteem, such as the composer Felix Mendelssohn, a significant contributor to the Romantic movement in music.

The principal difficulty that the prince had to contend with during the couple's first year of marriage had to do with statecraft. Victoria would not allow Albert to participate in government affairs. This exclusion may have been at the suggestion of Lord Melbourne, who was concerned about the manner in which his countrymen would react to a foreigner participating in British politics. Whatever the reason, however, Albert did not enjoy being kept at arm's length from affairs of state. Having no significant project that demanded his energies, he felt purposeless and unsatisfied. But the young man once again demonstrated his flexibility and sense of industry; denied access to statecraft, he involved himself in "domestic" management — he set about reorganizing Buckingham Palace.

The palace had become the epitome of mismanagement, disorganization, and waste. Duplication of services and an inefficient division of labor had made household functions cumbersome and awkward. One of the more humorous examples of this inefficiency involved the windows of the palace. One office was responsible for washing the insides of the windows, another office washed them on the outside. Rather than constantly spotless windows, this system resulted in windows that were always dirty — on one side or the other. Albert solved this and other problems that plagued the palace by creating a single, responsible office. He gained a considerable measure of attention and even respect for the highly efficient manner in which he had transformed the royal domestic scene, but he was still kept on the outside of British politics.

Finally the prince's difficult position was resolved

What a blessing it is I have now in my beloved Husband real and solid happiness, which no Politics, no worldly reverses can change. Kind and excellent as Lord M. [Melbourne] is, and kind as he was to me, in Society I had but amusement.
—QUEEN VICTORIA
in a letter to King Leopold I
of Belgium

by an act of nature — when Victoria became pregnant. The Privy Council was extremely mindful of the fact that Princess Charlotte had died in childbirth. Should such an event befall Victoria, her child would be under the protection of a regent. Tradition demanded that — foreigner or not — the prince be this regent. Victoria was finally compelled to involve Albert in affairs of state so that he would be better prepared to serve should such a tragedy occur.

In September 1840 Albert was sworn into the Privy Council, and began to study the law and constitution of England. In a short time, he began assuming an ever-larger share of the administrative work. Victoria came to trust and rely on him, and even the skeptical ministers quickly appreciated his intelligence and ability.

When Victoria's baby was born, the doctor quickly inspected it, found it healthy, and announced, "Oh, Madam, it is a princess." Victoria, who had hoped for a son, since British tradition dictates that when possible the throne will go to the first male child, responded, "Never mind, the next will be a prince."

The princess royal was named Victoria, but her family nickname — Pussy — was always used at home. Queen Victoria was unique in British history — not only was she queen regnant (a ruling queen), but a mother as well.

Albert assumed many of Victoria's duties during her long convalescence following the birth. Unlike Victoria, Albert was keenly aware of the serious social issues facing England at the time.

The 1830s had been a decade marked by sweeping social change and upheaval. Rapid industrial development had increased tensions between rich and poor, between owners and laborers. Benjamin Disraeli, later to become Victoria's trusted prime minister, called these classes the "two nations." There were numerous episodes of unrest, and the authorities rallied against anything they thought might become open rebellion. Forceful repression was used to deal with the discontent, but outcries for better representation and for human welfare mounted around the nation.

Easily the most extreme movement in England

Victoria (1840–1901), Queen Victoria's first daughter. The queen's pregnancy gave Albert, a German, the opportunity he wanted to become more involved in British political affairs; should the queen die during childbirth, it was thought, the prince consort must be capable of fulfilling his duties as regent.

THE BETTMANN ARCHIVE

Woodcut depicting children of the unemployed, sleeping on the street. Huge population increases and mass unemployment marked England's lurch into the modern age. Prince Albert's concern for the working classes prompted Queen Victoria to work harder for social reforms.

during this period was the Chartists. This movement was based on a "People's Charter" and its Six Points, written by the trade unionists William Lovett and Francis Place in 1838. Its membership was drawn from people of the lower-middle and working classes, who felt that the Reform Bill of 1832, a bill intended to increase democratic representation in local government, did not go far enough. The Chartists held mass demonstrations and drew up petitions. They called for the universal right to vote (though only for men), the abolition of the property ownership requirement for members of Parliament, and the holding of annual general elections. They wanted to do away with the aristocratic House of Lords as well as with the monarchy itself. In general, Chartism sought to establish direct, rather than parliamentary, democracy. Eventually, compromises to these radical demands were granted by both Liberals and Conservatives.

Many reforms came about as scientific knowledge and methods began to influence government. Rational thinking rather than emotional speech-making began to characterize governmental debates and decision-making; statistics became as important as oratory in Parliament. Difficulties brought about by an economy dependent upon factories and numerous city dwellers required swift, systematic solutions. Laws needed to be made to improve the lives of peasants-turned-machine-age-workers.

In 1832 the Poor Law Commission was established, and certain social services were then provided for the many unfortunate men, women, and children victimized by England's rapid industrialization. Famed novelist of the period, Charles Dickens, ridiculed Poor Law institutions such as the workhouse, where the poor labored in exchange for a subsistence diet and shelter. His novel *Oliver Twist* exposed the abuses suffered by children in the labor force.

The following years brought the Factory Act, inspired by utopian theorist Robert Owen and guided through Parliament by Antony Ashley Cooper, known as Lord Shaftesbury. Among other provisions, it made various types of child labor illegal, and required regular inspections of all textile mills. Lord Shaftesbury is credited with introducing the first factory laws; making laws to cope with the new "condition of England" was the political alternative to widespread violence. Under the Factory Act, children and adults were limited to working 10-hour days. A few hours each day were set aside for the children's education under the 1833 act. Shaftesbury also helped radicals such as Edwin Chadwick and his supporters in their efforts to upgrade public health and improve conditions for agricultural workers.

Another major cause of social change was the invention of the steam locomotive. Trains began to make city goods and services available to distant rural communities, while providing access to Great Britain's cities and towns that was undreamed of only years before. More than 50 railway acts were passed by Parliament by 1835; 39 more such bills followed two years later. As the railroads grew, so did the coal and iron businesses.

The railroad became a symbol of England's industrial growth in the art and literature of the period. Alfred Lord Tennyson, Victoria's poet laureate, seemed to sum up the meaning of progress to the Victorian age while aboard the first train on the Manchester and Liverpool Railway: "Let the great world spin forever down the ringing grooves of change."

As England's industries, railroads, and mines were increasing in importance, there were those who foresaw the stresses of rapid change. Philosophers — most notably John Stuart Mill — and labor reformers, such as Robert Owen (who also designed experimental communities) made significant contributions to the political and social questions of the day. Mill specifically addressed the issue of the freedom of the individual, and the extent to which that freedom may be compromised by the State for the general good.

Mill believed that the aim of government should be to secure happiness for the most people, and that this goal could only be accomplished if government did more rather than less. He supported trade

Never before had Victoria felt so acutely the necessity for doing her duty. She worked more methodically than ever at the business of state; she watched over her children with untiring vigilance. She carried on a large correspondence. She was occupied from morning to night.
—LYTTON STRACHEY
British historian writing about Victoria's first years of motherhood

unionism, and also helped to originate British socialist thought. Mill asserted very early that democracy was essential to human development.

Most owners and industrialists thought that the need for government regulation had been refuted long ago by the 18th-century economist Adam Smith in his *The Wealth of Nations*, published in 1776. However, by the mid-1840s, as the historian G. M. Young explains, "it was becoming evident that the line between what the State may do and what it must leave alone had been drawn in the wrong place. . . ."

As new industries grew, they brought increased job opportunities to the cities, and people flocked to urban areas to find work. The proportion of people who made a living from farming or livestock began to shrink as factories and towns grew with amazing speed. This energetic economy promoted the growth of a new, largely urban middle class. However, in many places industrial growth occurred more rapidly than urban development could keep pace with, resulting in housing shortages, crowding, filth, and dire poverty. Industrialization developed erratically and at an uneven pace. With it came a startling new phenomenon: mass unemployment.

As the number of people and conditions changed, so too did their attitudes and ideas. The most frequent and urgent demand was for enlargement of the franchise — the categories of people who were permitted to vote.

Although such affairs had never seemed crucial to Victoria before, Albert's interests became her own. In a manner that was typical of Victoria's earnest devotion, she wholeheartedly supported and adopted Albert's views and interests regarding social reform. Together they influenced and inspired many of the changes that accompanied England's industrialization.

It was during this time that Lord Melbourne's position as a Whig prime minister finally became untenable. Melbourne, while an excellent tutor to Victoria in many respects, had an almost cavalier disregard for the plight of the poor in general and the Irish in particular. As a result, he airily passed

We are living at a period of most wonderful transition, which tends rapidly to accomplish this great end to which indeed all history points—the realization of the unity of mankind.
—PRINCE ALBERT
a few weeks before the
opening of the Great Exhibition

over their concerns when educating or advising Victoria, which left her with a very distorted view of how the majority of her subjects lived.

Albert changed all this. Genuinely concerned for the welfare of the working class, he brought these ugly conditions to Victoria's attention and urged that suitable reforms be made.

In 1841 Sir Robert Peel replaced Melbourne as prime minister. This time the transition was smooth, largely due to Albert's discretion in handling the matter. The prince had always maintained that the Crown should be above partisan involvement in national politics and that the royal household should be representative of both parties. Victoria deferred to his opinion.

Meanwhile, Melbourne advised Peel on how to treat the queen in order to secure and maintain amicable relations with her. In addition to Lord M.'s coaching, Peel enjoyed another advantage that he had not had previously — he now had a powerful ally in Albert. The prince respected Peel's ability and shrewdness, and his recommendations did much to change Victoria's opinion of her new prime minister.

A cotton inspection station in New Orleans, Louisiana. Importing high quality cotton from the southern United States allowed the British textile industry to become a major power in the world fabric market.

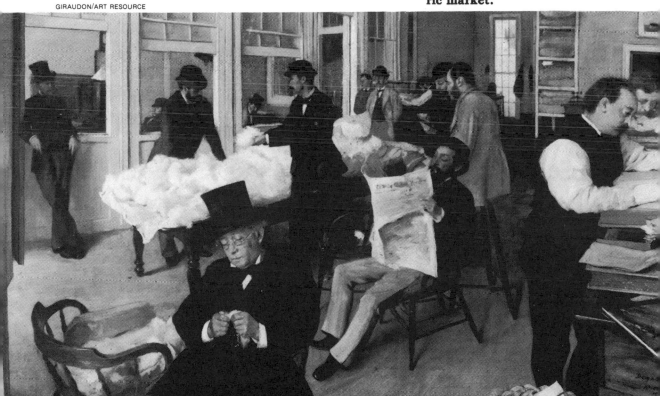

London poor in Whitechapel, a working-class area of the English capital. During the Industrial Revolution people seeking jobs flocked to the cities, which in many cases did not have the services to deal with the huge influx.

These many positive factors made Victoria's parting from Lord Melbourne a great deal less painful. Peel was quite different from Lord Melbourne. A member of the new middle class, Peel's wealth was not the result of hereditary position; his grandfather had founded the family fortune in England's cotton industry. Sir Robert, therefore, had a very practical approach to economic and political concerns. Not surprisingly, his ministry introduced many social reforms. He was responsible for many of the changes made in the areas of trade and banking, two of which had lasting impacts upon the English economy — the promotion of free trade and the introduction of a graduated income tax.

His unceasing efforts to enact such changes illustrates Peel's keen awareness of the distress of the working class. By promoting free trade, the entire economy became stronger and more active, resulting in decreases in the general cost of living. Peel accomplished this by repealing tariffs and duties on imports. The Corn Laws, which established restrictions on agricultural trade, were repealed during "the hungry forties," when harvests and foreign trade were depressed. Furthermore, the graduated income tax served to reduce the taxation of the poor by shifting a higher burden of the cost to the extremely wealthy. As might be expected, not everyone welcomed such changes, but Peel's dedication and ability, combined with the unflagging support of the royal couple, made him a virtually unstoppable political force.

Meanwhile, Victoria's family continued to grow with almost alarming speed. In 1841 Victoria had a second child, and this time it was a boy — the heir that England had been longing for. This child, the Prince of Wales, was named Albert Edward (or "Bertie" as he was nicknamed). He would become King Edward VII and would rule from 1901 to 1910. Victoria and Albert were so delighted by the prospect of their growing family that they eventually had seven more children. They were acutely concerned with their children's growth, health, and education.

It was this concern that led to a major alteration in the household's nursery. Albert frequently found himself in disagreement with Victoria's former governess, Baroness Lehzen, regarding the children's health. Their relationship deteriorated steadily until Albert finally expressed his feelings to Victoria, saying that he doubted if it were wise to allow Baroness Lehzen to continue to oversee the nursery.

Although this incident generated considerable emotion, Victoria finally released her old governess from service, doing so tactfully and gently. She received a handsome pension and went home to Germany. Without Baroness Lehzen's distrustful warnings in her ear and with Conroy out of the picture, Victoria listened ever more closely to Al-

Painting of a wheat field on the Isle of Wight. This island off the southeast coast of England was the location of the royal family's Osborne House, which they purchased in 1843.

bert's advice, and closed the gap between herself and her mother. The queen's capacity for forgiveness was at least as great as her capacity for dislike and distrust, and soon she forgave the duchess for all that had passed before.

While they were still young, the children had plenty of time for the gaieties of life that came with living in Buckingham Palace. One such festive occasion was Christmas, and the associated German traditions that Albert maintained in his new homeland. One tradition in particular was to catch on not only in England, but the United States as well. At Christmas, the royal family would decorate a pine tree in their living room, covering it with baubles and candles, and surrounding it with presents. Their English subjects followed their example in growing numbers, quickly adopting this as a delightful new custom of their own.

Even though Buckingham Palace was large enough for any growing family, Victoria and Albert also decided to purchase a home of their own. Using funds that were largely garnered through Albert's prudent reorganization of the Buckingham household, they were able to buy a property in 1843 on the Isle of Wight — Osborne House. This became a permanent holiday home for their family, and since a new railway line had linked nearby Portsmouth with London, the sovereign could return to the seat of government rapidly should an emergency arise. Osborne House afforded them an opportunity to live a more informal, private life, and Albert rearranged the grounds and buildings to reflect this atmosphere. When visited today, Osborne still retains a homey feeling.

Another favorite diversion of the royal family was to take trips to Scotland, though time constraints made these sojourns rarer than their visits to Osborne. Consequently, they spent their longer holidays in the Highlands, where they bought a small castle — Balmoral. Once again, the prince redesigned the castle, not only expanding it, but making it a suitable place for their ministers to stay.

Both Victoria and Albert loved the Highlands best of all, since it was here that they had the greatest degree of freedom. Albert found the wild, rugged beauty of the countryside reminiscent of his German homeland and would spend hours hiking and shooting. Victoria enjoyed endless picnics with the children and pony-cart rides that took them around the countryside. During such trips, the queen met many of the common folk of the country, and found the unaffected demeanor of the Highlanders a refreshing change from court life. She was briefly able to forget that she was a queen. Having found great happiness and freedom in these days, Victoria eventually wrote a book about them entitled *Leaves from the Journal of Our Life in the Highlands.*

Meanwhile, the unstoppable force of Prime Minister Peel had met with an immovable object. Having convinced Victoria and Albert of the desperate need for free trade, Peel had been able to modify or rework virtually every area that the old tariffs affected except one — the Corn Laws. These laws made it illegal to import corn (the British term for grain) if prices were too low, thus protecting England's agricultural production from foreign competitors who could sell their corn more cheaply.

In 1845 these restrictions became the subject of heated debate. That year, England had a terrible summer which destroyed the corn harvest. To make matters worse, Ireland lost its potato crop. The need for foreign corn, particularly in famine-stricken Ireland, reached crisis proportions. Peel launched himself into the midst of this fray with customary dedication, fighting passionately for the repeal of the Corn Laws. After a bitter fight, he succeeded in getting the bill passed into law, but the fierce opposition that the issue generated had split his own party, undermining his power as prime minister. He resigned his post in 1846.

Victoria and her husband had worked well with Prime Minister Peel, despite the Tory's ardent desire for reforms, since he accorded the royal couple all the respect and deference that their positions deserved. However, the role of the constitutional monarchy was still undergoing change, not just in England but throughout Europe.

Constant subtle alterations, redefinitions, and

> *Countrybred men live by custom, and in the new environment custom was killed and habit shaken.*
> —DAVID THOMSON
> British historian, describing the social effects of the Industrial Revolution

challenges were relentlessly chipping away at the power of sovereigns everywhere. On the continent, this often exploded into nationalist movements, political turmoil, and even revolt. Not only was the map of Europe changing, but so were the attitudes and beliefs of its many peoples.

Naturally, this was of great concern to Victoria and Albert, who wanted to preserve the monarchy as a viable form of government. Not only did this represent their own interests, but those of their families, since they were related to many of the crowned heads of Europe.

After Peel's resignation, the next ministry was headed by Lord John Russell, but he was not the most newsworthy member of Victoria's government. This time, it was the foreign minister, Lord Palmerston, who was responsible for the most serious political clashes. Palmerston's politics were diametrically opposed to Victoria and Albert's. His sympathies were with what he considered to be the oppressed peoples of Europe. Palmerston was a practical man who held progressive views; Albert was essentially conservative, but also rather idealistic. Victoria had not been aware of Palmerston's beliefs when she had first encountered him during his tenure as Lord Melbourne's foreign secretary. Immensely popular even then, Palmerston had had little interaction with the young Victoria, mostly due to the fact that Melbourne acted as a buffer, and because her own views on foreign affairs were as yet largely unformed. Now, however, Victoria and Palmerston were face to face, and there were constant, bitter disagreements.

Palmerston was an astute observer of the political scene and had no personal reason to be particularly for or against the monarchy. He saw that changes were coming, and that, given the ongoing evolution of social and political values, it was extremely dangerous to obstruct such changes; stubborn rulers had often been the cause of bloody revolutions. Moreover, Palmerston felt that the majority of the changes that were being demanded were as reasonable as they were necessary, and thus he often failed to observe the strict neutrality his post demanded.

But Palmerston's distaste for monarchical powers did not end with his actions abroad; they spilled over into his dealings with the queen. Not wishing to be hampered by constant political and personal conflicts, Palmerston frequently acted without informing Victoria of his intentions. On several occasions, he acted upon extremely urgent and sensitive matters without consulting her or even the prime minister.

Victoria, as may well be imagined, was furious at what she considered a near-treasonous disregard for the authority of the Crown. Palmerston, however, considered himself primarily answerable to Parliament. In this age of change, there were enough people who agreed with him to make it all but impossible for Victoria to do anything about his behavior. While he certainly could have been more tactful and respectful, the foreign minister made it clear that the power of decision was in his hands and not hers, setting a new precedent that further eroded the prerogatives and power of the English monarchy.

As prime minister, Lord John Russell was in a

In this political cartoon, starving Irish peasants line the coast, beseeching American ships for help. The failure of the potato crop in 1846 led to widespread famine and the death of nearly 250,000 peasants.

most unenviable position between the two bitterly opposed combatants. Victoria was constantly railing about the foreign minister's impudence and disrespect, and while Russell may have agreed on many points, he was powerless to do anything about it. Palmerston's popularity had grown immensely, and as a result, he had too much support in the House of Commons for Russell to ask for his resignation.

Eventually, however, Palmerston crossed the fine line he had been treading. In 1848 revolution swept through Paris. Famine had broken out in France the previous year, and English bankers had withdrawn funds, worsening the French economic crisis. King Louis Philippe refused to ease the plight of the hungry workers. When the revolutionaries took over Paris, Louis Philippe was forced to flee, while the rebels declared France a republic. On December 10, that same year, Louis Napoleon (or Napoleon III, third son of Louis Bonaparte, brother of Napoleon I) had been elected president of the new French Republic, but when he discovered that the constitution did not permit him to run for a second term, he proclaimed himself emperor. Shortly after this 1851 *coup d'état*, or takeover of the state, Palmerston guaranteed the new emperor British support without first securing official sanction from Parliament or the Crown. Russell and Victoria had had enough of Palmerston's disrespect for authority, and now had sufficient grounds to call for his resignation.

Palmerston satisfied them by quitting his post as foreign minister, but this was not the end of his political adventures. His next tenure in office was as home secretary, a position which rarely brought him into contact with the queen. Furthermore, Victoria's interest in the doings of the ministry was considerably less passionate than her interest in foreign relations, so the friction between them subsided.

Not all the accomplishments of this period were political, however. Prince Albert also kindled Victoria's interest in another important project, one which illustrated his belief — and pride — in Britain's industrialization. Albert was fascinated by

It was such a time of pleasure, of pride, of satisfaction & of deep thankfulness, it is the triumph of peace and good will towards all. To see this wonderful Exhibition which has pleased everyone looked upon as dearest Albert's work, this has, & does make me happy.
—QUEEN VICTORIA
writing in her journal,
July 18, 1851

every new scientific discovery, and had had no difficulty in convincing Victoria to share this interest. The grand result of this mutual interest was the Great Exhibition of 1851.

Albert was both mastermind and architect of this huge undertaking, a forum in which to exhibit Britain's most recent revolutions in science, technology, and art. In short order, his scheme grew to encompass technological accomplishments from around the world. The Great Exhibition was held inside a huge palace of glass that was specially constructed in London's Hyde Park. The "Crystal Palace," as it was called by local newspapers, covered 26 acres, housing 14,000 exhibits from all over the world. The theme of the exhibition was the modern age. Beauty and practicality, art and science, were blended to-

Women digging a field for a crop of potatoes in Roscommon County, Ireland. Since both Ireland and England were suffering from severe food shortages, Prime Minister Robert Peel attained the repeal of the Corn Laws, which had mandated high tariffs on the import of foreign grains.

The Crystal Palace in London was specially built to house the "Great Exhibition of 1851." Spearheaded by Prince Albert, the exhibition was intended to put the "modern age" on view for visitors from around the world and, especially for the English, to offer a promising glimpse of better times to come.

gether into a glittering testimonial to the ingenuity of man and the new age into which he was entering.

The queen opened the Great Exhibition on May 1, 1851, and recorded in her journal, "This day is one of the greatest and most glorious days of our lives, with which, to my pride and joy, the name of my dearly beloved Albert is forever associated!"

The exhibition was a great success. Visitors came from all over the world, traveling hundreds of miles to view the exhibits. Perhaps more significantly, it also attracted huge throngs of working men and women, who were shuttled in from all over England by special trains. To everyone, but to the working class in particular, the Great Exhibition offered not only a chance to behold the wonders of the age, but a glimpse of times to come — times that would be brighter and more hopeful.

But to the surprise of many, pride and confidence weren't the only benefits generated by the Great Exhibition. When it closed in October, it had made a tremendous profit. Albert proposed to Parliament that the exhibition should be extended, given a permanent form. He suggested that the proceeds be used to buy a large plot of land in Kensington, on which educational institutions would be founded and built. His proposal was carried unanimously by Parliament.

Although somewhat changed and modified as the years went by, Albert's plans carried through. The list of colleges and museums that now occupy the Kensington property is extensive. It includes the Imperial College, the City and Guilds College of Engineering, the Royal College of Music, the Natural History Museum, the Science Museum, and the Victoria and Albert Museum.

If Albert's adopted nation had any lingering doubts regarding his competence, dedication, ingenuity, or strength of character, they were now dispelled. In the face of enormous difficulties and considerable opposition, the prince had orchestrated a success of unequalled magnitude.

Happiest of all was Victoria, who felt that finally her beloved Albert had received the recognition he so richly deserved. Her unbounded joy was evident as she wrote, "Albert's dearest name is immortalized with this great conception, *his* own, and *my* own dear country showed she was worthy of it."

The queen and the prince consort among their subjects. Albert, whose German ancestry had at first caused problems for him with some of the English, convinced his adopted country, through his involvement with the Great Exhibition and other gestures, that his dedication was genuine.

4

War and Death

During the 1850s, a new international worry had begun to receive the attention of a number of European powers: the threat of Russian expansion. For many years, the Turkish Ottoman Empire had been a strong bulwark against the forces of the tsar, but now that empire was growing feeble and the governments of both Britain and France feared that Russian forces might attempt to occupy lands that had formerly been under Turkish dominion. In particular, they dreaded the possibility that the Russians might seize the strategically critical Dardanelles, the strait that controls the passageway to and from the Black Sea.

The first moves in this game of international chess occurred in 1853, when Russia invaded Moldavia and Wallachia (two principalities along the Danube River) on the dubious grounds that they were protecting the religious right of Russians living there. Britain and France communicated their displeasure to the tsar, adding that Turkey had their support in this matter and that the Turkish empire had every right to declare war on Russia. Shortly thereafter, the Russian fleet sailed from its

THE BETTMANN ARCHIVE

Alfred Tennyson (1809–92), the famous poet of the Victorian age. His poem, "The Charge of the Light Brigade," immortalized the soldiers who gave their lives in these words: "Theirs not to reason why,/ Theirs but to do and die./ Into the valley of Death/ Rode the six hundred."

Russian illustration depicting Russian troops fighting at Sevastopol during the Crimean War (1853–56). Britain and France sent their forces to this naval base after Russian military provocations against the Ottoman Empire of Turkey made defense of the region an imperative for the two western European powers.

Black Sea port in Sevastopol on the Crimean Peninsula and destroyed the Turkish fleet in the harbor of Sinope. International pressure rose, and then boiled over. In February 1854 Britain and France declared war on Russia and sent troops to occupy the Crimea.

Victoria was filled with national pride and visions of glory in battle. She believed that hers was the finest army in the world, and based on past accomplishments, she had every reason to hold this belief. It was, incidentally, a belief shared by the army itself. The truth proved to be a bitter and bloody disappointment.

After 40 years of relative peace in Europe, the British army had fallen into a state of complacent disrepair. Inefficiency was common, supplies were inadequate, and equipment was outdated. On the Crimean battlefront shortages of clothing, transport, and medical supplies led to confusion, defeat, and ultimately, terrible suffering.

Blame for the war was pinned on the tsar, Nicholas I. Queen Victoria felt gripped by suspense, and was frustrated by a lack of trustworthy information about the war's progress. For a time the war was an intensely popular one with the people of Britain. Very soon, however, they were not to be spared a single detail as the whole shocking story unfolded; for the first time in its distinguished history, *The Times* of London had sent a war correspondent to the front lines. This correspondent, William Howard Russell, effectively conveyed his sense of horror and outrage to readers back in England, stunning them with graphic accounts of the miseries suffered by the troops of the "world's finest army." The panic of battle, the dull ache of retreat, the gory horrors of field surgery — he captured every brutal detail of the Crimean War. The English had known other military disasters, some worse than this, but never had there been someone at the front, filling daily eyewitness reports of the ghastly events that transpired there.

In January 1855 Lord Palmerston was appointed prime minister. This time, he and the queen were in agreement — they both wanted a victory in the

Half a league, half a league,
Half a league onward,
All in the valley of Death
Rode the six hundred.
"Forward the Light Brigade!
Charge for the guns!" he said.
Into the valley of Death
Rode the six hundred.

—ALFRED LORD TENNYSON
British poet laureate, in
"The Charge of the Light Brigade"

Crimea, and as quickly as possible. What they did not agree on was the role of the press. Palmerston's opinion was that the newspaper reports' negative impact on the nation was offset by the "great advantages." Victoria remained skeptical of Palmerston's belief in free speech.

The fighting centered in Sevastopol, the heavily fortified base of the Russian fleet. Perhaps the most famous incident of the entire tragic war was the heroic but costly charge of the Light Brigade. Over two-thirds of the approximately 600 British cavalry soldiers who stormed a Russian stronghold were needlessly killed during the battle of Balaklava. The chief cause of the tragedy was the stubbornness and rivalry of two high-ranking British officers. In 1854 the British poet Tennyson immortalized the futility and horror of the battle in his famous poem "The Charge of the Light Brigade."

The other heroic story of the war originated not on the battlefield but in the tents of the wounded and the sick. Florence Nightingale and her nurses revolutionized the concept of army medicine, providing many forms of medical care that doctors had too little time to offer. Nightingale fought not only against the horrors of pain and death on the battlefield, but against prejudice and mistrust from doctors and a society that thought it improper or dangerous to have women ministering to the sick on the battlefront. Victoria was particularly appreciative of Nightingale's efforts. She was appalled at the stories of her soldiers' sufferings, and reacted

THE BETTMANN ARCHIVE

Zouaves — Algerians conscripted by the French from their North African colony — were adept at making *gabions*, a type of basket or cage filled with rocks or earth and used as a building support. The Zouaves were later brought to the Crimea to assist in the battle against the Russians.

67

to news of Florence Nightingale's noble work with profuse praise and statements of support, thereby silencing a great many of the nurse's adversaries.

Throughout the Crimean War, Victoria displayed what seemed to be mixed, sometimes contradictory, attitudes. On one hand, she was filled with martial fervor, lost in fantasies of the glories of war and the nobility of sacrifice for the empire. On the other hand, she was aghast at the misery and agony that her troops suffered, wishing above all else to resolve the war quickly and with as little loss of life as possible. Both her warlike dreams and her earnest compassion were honest feelings that arose from her heart. Characteristically, she refused to forsake one approach in order to adopt the other, but instead accepted them both without question. Her spirit was both hawk and dove, warrior and healer.

The Russian fleet destroyed the Turkish fleet at Sinope on the Black Sea in late 1853. The attack heightened the international tensions that led Britain and France formally to declare war on Russia early the next year.

But the participants in the war did not have the inclination, much less the luxury, of indulging in the same fantasies that occupied Victoria's mind. Sevastopol finally fell, but to Victoria's disappointment this battle was actually won by Britain's allies, the French. Russian influence in the Black Sea was curtailed, peace was declared in 1856 — an indecisive outcome that England called a "victory." The Russians would become militarily active against Turkey in 1876. As it turned out, the only people who emerged from this horrible war with any praise or glory were the common soldiers and the nurses. A special medal called the Victoria Cross was struck for the veterans of the Crimean campaign. The queen saw fit to overlook the usual bounds of protocol for which her era was known and personally decorated the officers and enlisted men alike. She

was later touched to hear that the men had not even wanted to part with their medals for engraving because they feared that they might not get back the same medal she had handed them.

But the bloodshed did not end; it simply relocated. In May 1857 England received news of troubles in India. At first the reports were sporadic and uncertain, but within weeks, the reports were clear: the East India Company's *sepoy*, meaning native, troops had mutinied.

For years British forces in India had been responsible for widespread conquest and annexation. The British imposed their own systems of administration and education on the conquered regions, enforcing regulations that conflicted with India's religions and customs. Laws were instituted to eliminate those customs or practices that the British considered uncivilized or hostile. For instance, the British made illegal the killing of female infants, an age-old custom among Indian peasant families, and *suttee*, a ritual whereby a man's widow and mistresses threw themselves on his funeral pyre.

News of massacres and atrocities against Europeans filled the English with horror and rage. By

Night attack during the Crimean War. Terrible suffering marked the fighting, as British forces experienced shortages of food, clothing, and medical supplies. Queen Victoria was of two minds about the war — aghast at her troops' misery but dearly wanting a glorious military victory.

mid-1859 it became clear that the mutiny had been quelled, but it was not soon to be forgotten. Many English were never able to forgive the Indians for what they considered a barbaric act of treason, holding a vindictive grudge against the sepoys and all Indians for a long time.

The mutiny had brought another issue forward: the ability of the East India Company to adequately govern its Indian holdings. Prior to the Sepoy Mutiny, control of India had been shared by the company and the British government. The former had maintained its own army, navy, and tax collection service, and over a 20-year period, had doubled the amount of territory it held through shrewd bargaining and aggressive tactics. However, even before the mutiny, there was some worry that the company had overexpanded, and the possibility of transferring all powers of government to the Crown had received serious consideration. The Indian mutiny served to confirm the necessity of this move, and within months, the queen and her government had assumed full control of India. This transfer was effected by an act of Parliament entitled the New India Bill, which was submitted to Victoria and Albert for inspection. They were alarmed at the harsh, vengeful tone of the document, which spoke of the queen's power "for the undermining of native religions and customs." Victoria and Albert suggested extensive changes, in light of their concern that "such a document should breathe feelings of generosity, benevolence, and religious toleration."

Though Victoria had been every bit as horrified as her subjects at the atrocities and bloodshed of the rebellion, she maintained an excellent sense of balance throughout that period, realizing that the fault lay not just with the rebellious Indians, but with the oppressive system of government to which they had been subject. Therefore, when the bloodshed ceased, she showed a spirit of forgiveness and even conciliation that few of her fellow countrymen displayed.

By the time the New India Bill passed in 1858, the ministry had changed again. The Conservatives (formerly the Tories) were in power again. This time

I cannot say how touched and impressed I have been by the sight of these noble, brave, & so sadly wounded men & how anxious I feel to be of use to them, & to try & get some employment for those who are maimed for life.
—QUEEN VICTORIA
writing in her journal after visiting wounded British soldiers, February 1855

Lord Derby was prime minister, and the clever Benjamin Disraeli wrote to Victoria regarding the bill, suggesting a new way to govern India. His letter pointed out that the New India Bill was ". . . only the ante-chamber of an imperial palace, and your Majesty would do well to deign to consider steps which are now necessary to influence the opinions, and affect the imaginations of the Indian populations. The name of your Majesty ought to be impressed upon their native life." Later on, Victoria would remember these words as she lobbied to become empress of India.

It seemed to Victoria that she had barely finished with childbearing and empire building when the marriages of her children became a concern. In 1858, the queen's oldest daughter Vicky (or Pussy) was married to Prince Frederick William of Prussia. The young prince (who was called Fritz by the family) had met Vicky when he had come to England for the opening of the Great Exhibition in 1851, and they had liked each other immediately. When he visited the family again in 1855, a romance developed and he had asked the royal parents for their permission to seek her hand in marriage. Albert and Victoria were delighted, but because of Vicky's youth (she was only 14 at the time), the betrothal remained a secret. However, she and Fritz, completely in love and devoted to each other, were finally

Queen Victoria and Prince Albert in 1854. The photograph was taken by Roger Fenton, British photography pioneer, best known for his Crimean War photographs.

Queen Victoria with her granddaughter, also named Victoria, who was the daughter of Princess Alice (1843–78). By the late 1850s the queen had given birth to the last of her nine children and began to think about suitable mates for the older ones. Her daughters Alice and Vicky both married German noblemen.

married in 1858. Although the experience of watching a daughter get married was in no way as painful as giving birth to one, it was nevertheless a day of enormous anxiety for Victoria.

Victoria might have been even more anxious had she known how historically important the wedding would ultimately be. Fritz, nephew of the king of Prussia and heir to the throne, was to deliver a powerful nation into the hands of his eldest son, who was born in 1859. That eldest son was William II, first grandson of Victoria, and eventually the kaiser of World War I Germany.

But for now, the most remarkable thing about the birth was that it made Victoria not just queen of England and mother of nine, but a grandmother as well — all by age 40.

Roger Fenton photograph of British soldiers in the Crimea. The most famous engagement of the war occurred during the Anglo-French siege of Sevastopol, with the "charge of the light brigade" — an all-out assault on Russian fortifications that, while valiant, resulted in the slaughter of many British cavalrymen.

The Victorian period saw Britain establish industrial progress at home (without experiencing a revolution) and a vast empire abroad. Many Englishmen became complacent and self-satisfied. Smug contentment even reached the chambers of Parliament. Lord Palmerston remarked before one session ". . . we cannot go on legislating forever." His comment reflected the widely held belief that little remained to be done. England was not without critics, however. Many British intellectuals scrutinized Victorian society and did not always like what they saw. The economist Walter Bagehot wrote: "A sense of satisfaction permeates the country because most of the country feels it has got the precise thing that suits it." He went on to note that, in the 1860s, any Englishman wishing to voice a complaint would have been completely ignored.

Charles Dickens often made sharp observations in his satirical novels. In *Hard Times*, published in 1854, Dickens portrays a typical official telling schoolchildren that only factual knowledge is useful and practical, while any other kind is mere "fancy": "'You are to be in all things regulated and governed,' said the gentleman, 'by fact. We hope to have before long, a board of fact, composed of commissioners of fact, who will force the people to be a people of fact, and nothing but fact.' " This point of view was often found among reformers and educators as well as businessmen who had been influenced by utilitarian thinkers. John Stuart Mill's father, James Mill, along with his friend Jeremy Bentham, helped develop utilitarianism. The elder Mill had taught his son from an early age nothing but factual information and discouraged fantasy.

The Sepoy Rebellion, 1857–59. Sepoys, native Indian troops enlisted by Britain's East India Company, staged a prolonged mutiny against British rule following widespread rumors that they had been using rifle cartridges greased in the fat of cows and pigs — the former animal sacred to Hindus, the latter abhorrent to Muslims.

THE BETTMANN ARCHIVE

This humorous — but all-too-serious — illustration shows a stern Queen Victoria admonishing her son, Albert Edward (1841–1910) — affectionately known as Bertie — for his indiscretions, which taxed his father's already failing health. Albert would succeed his mother on the throne in 1901 as King Edward VII.

The Scottish essayist Thomas Carlyle, who supported the Chartist movement, fiercely denounced the era for its materialist values. Carlyle was thoroughly outraged by the inequities and injustices around him, and sympathized with radicals who wanted to abolish poverty through drastic reform. John Ruskin, possibly the greatest social critic of the Victorian age, objected, like Carlyle, to British society's emphasis on class divisions and competitive economics.

In terms of scientific and political thought, the year 1859 was a significant one for the future as well as for Victorian England. Charles Darwin published his *Origin of Species* after 25 years of research. This work introduced the theory of evolution by natural selection, which shook traditional religious explanations of how life on earth came to exist. Darwin stated that all species — including man — resulted from gradual changes that oc-

I am anxious to repeat one thing, and that one is my firm resolve, my irrevocable decision, that his wishes—his plans—about everything, his views about everything are to be my law!

—QUEEN VICTORIA
to King Leopold I after
Albert's death

curred among generations of organisms in their struggle to survive.

A work that proved especially popular that same year was *Self-Help*, by Samuel Smiles. Smiles argued that life was not barbaric in a free enterprise economy (as Matthew Arnold would later suggest); he claimed that "a rational code of duty" stopped society from becoming anarchy. Victorian morality had thus been defined. Smiles had many imitators whose preachings gained followers among the middle classes, who were eager to believe that material riches were the reward for virtues such as thrift and hard work.

Matthew Arnold's *Culture and Anarchy* appeared 10 years later. Perhaps the harshest attacks on materialist values, moral hypocrisy, and on the aristocratic classes were penned by Arnold. He accused

Among Victoria's contemporaries was Charles Dickens (1812–70), the celebrated English novelist and social critic. The author of such classics as *David Copperfield* and *Bleak House* also backed radical reforms aimed at countering government inefficiency, corruption, and the general poverty afflicting much of England at the time.

Victorian culture of actually creating anarchy while only *appearing* to be highly organized and stable. Its "worship" of machinery and what he called "collision," or systems based on conflict and competition, were barbaric, according to Arnold.

Victoria's life took a sharp downward plunge in 1861. The first disaster of that year was the death of her mother, the duchess of Kent. The estrangement that had marked their relationship early in Victoria's reign had been entirely reconciled, largely due to an illness the duchess suffered in 1859. This malady had awakened Victoria's deep sympathy, and she had put aside whatever small barriers lay between herself and her mother. Consequently, when the duchess fell ill again and died two years later, the queen was overcome with grief and remorse for the years when they had been "most wickedly estranged," by John Conroy and others. Victoria found comfort in Albert, who shared in her sorrow.

John Ruskin (left; 1819–1900), English art critic and author, with Dante Gabriel Rossetti (1828–82), English poet and painter, in 1863. Both were leading cultural figures of the Victorian Age; Ruskin also preached about the need for reforms in education and employment and established a charitable foundation that still exists.

John Stuart Mill (1806–73) was an English philosopher who protested against many conventional British social and intellectual practices. Mill also called for such reforms as universal suffrage and compulsory education long before many of his contemporaries.

Soon after, Victoria's firstborn son, the Prince of Wales, engaged in an indiscreet affair with an actress while serving with the British army in Ireland. The relationship did not last long, but became widely known, and many began to fear that the next heir to the throne would bring back the disgraceful ways of his earlier Hanoverian predecessors.

Prince Albert, already badly overworked and suffering from rheumatic pains and insomnia, nevertheless went to see young Prince Bertie, who was now at Cambridge University. Bertie's regrets and apologies were as sincere as they were profuse, and Albert returned reassured that Bertie's affair had been merely a fling, and not a foreshadowing of a licentious life. But Victoria noticed that the crisis had made Albert's rheumatism and insomnia even worse.

GIRAUDON/ART RESOURCE

Louis Pasteur (1822–95). The French chemist is best known for his pioneering work that led to the development of food "pasteurization." Pasteur's contributions inspired English surgeon Joseph Lister (1827–1912) to develop antiseptic surgery, an enormous gain for modern medicine.

Despite his condition, Albert involved himself in yet another crisis that demanded delicate handling, one that could have had grave international consequences, had it been mishandled. The incident involved the seizure of a British ship, the *Trent*, by an American man-of-war.

It must be remarked that very little was needed to trigger feelings of antipathy between the United States and Britain. Since the American Revolution of 1776, Anglo-American relations had been strained at best. More fuel was added to the fire by England's unsuccessful attempt to disrupt the new American republic during the War of 1812.

Across the Atlantic, the United States had become a divided nation and the American Civil War erupted in April 1861. The northern Union government headed by President Abraham Lincoln now was battling the Confederate southern states to prevent them from forming a separate country. Because of its interests in importing cotton from the South to manufacture cloth, and its friction with the Union government, Britain initially sympathized with the South, but officially maintained a position of strict neutrality.

However, when two Southern envoys tried sailing from Cuba to Britain aboard the English ship *Trent*, a Northern man-of-war intercepted and boarded the vessel and forcibly seized the two Confederate diplomats. When news of this reached London, many powerful persons were infuriated. The foreign office proposed sending a strongly worded memorandum to Washington, a memorandum that Prince Albert felt sure would lead to war, so inflammatory was its language. The Union government was already dismayed and angered by British sympathy for the South.

Albert redrafted the statement to create a masterpiece of diplomacy. The wording and tone were later to appear tactful and somewhat conciliatory, yet the memorandum clearly requested that the envoys be returned to English custody. The Union gov-

Charles Darwin (1809–82), English naturalist and author of *The Origin of Species* (1859) and *The Descent of Man* (1871). The theories of "survival of the fittest" and human evolution presented in these works sparked a worldwide furor — both religious and scientific — but are now widely accepted.

A cartoon depicting England's paternalistic view of the American republic. When the U.S. Civil War broke out in 1861 it was Prince Albert's masterful diplomacy that avoided an Anglo-American war as well; unfortunately, his round-the-clock efforts proved so strenuous for him that his health finally failed, and he died later in the year.

ernment received the memorandum, considered it carefully, and finally returned the envoys. Albert had rightly guessed that the last thing that the Union wanted was another war at sea and was willing to return the envoys if it were possible to do so with dignity. The entire incident faded and was forgotten. Confederate leaders had hoped that Britain's dependency on Southern cotton would bring the nation into an alliance with the South. Textile mills did close down in the Manchester and Lancashire areas, but the cotton shortage was not enough to make Britain enter the confict.

It is ironic that this great act of Prince Albert — arguably his greatest — was also his last. His day-and-night efforts in the *Trent* affair had taken a great toll on his already failing health. Towards the end of the incident, he confessed to Victoria that he felt so fatigued that he could barely hold a pen. His doctors became seriously alarmed.

Albert's illness spread with alarming swiftness. The doctors long refrained from mentioning the possibility of typhoid, the disease that had recently struck down the Spanish royal family, but as time progressed it grew obvious that this, in fact, was Albert's affliction. A painful time of seesawing hope and despair followed, as Albert would first gain some ground and then lose it. The strain on Victoria was enormous as she feared the loss of her great love, her confidant, her friend, her adviser.

On the morning of December 14, 1861, the doctors examined Albert and were happy to report that he might be improving. By the evening of that same day, the prince's condition had completely deteriorated. He died in the company of his family at the age of 42. Victoria was in a state of shock, until one of the doctors gave her a mild sedative. Then came a seemingly unending stream of anguished tears. Her sobbing finally exhausted her and she drifted into sleep.

Victoria and Albert in the late 1850s. Albert's death caused the queen to lapse into a state of depression that lasted for months.

5

The Mire of Grief

> *My life as a happy one has ended! The world is gone for me!*
> —QUEEN VICTORIA
> after Albert's death

Albert's death plunged Victoria into a period of seemingly bottomless grief. His sudden and unexpected demise had not only been a terrible shock, but had robbed Victoria of her optimism and happiness. Her despair was so extreme and so unrelenting that a modern diagnosis would probably indicate that the shock had caused her to suffer a nervous breakdown. Victoria grew very inactive and withdrawn, feeling that any joy in life had ended for her. She spoke only of her expectation of, and longing for, death.

Her sorrow was compounded by the fact that she ruled alone and unaided, swamped by an ever-increasing flood of paperwork. She came to realize, more than ever before, just how much she had depended on Albert, how he had been responsible for many of the Crown's administrative duties. He had been tireless in his drafting of memoranda, replies to dispatches, and correspondence with ministers. The enormous task of governing her empire alone suddenly loomed large before Victoria, leading her to self-doubts.

With an enormous effort, she managed to con-

THE BETTMANN ARCHIVE

Queen Victoria at her spinning wheel, around 1863. Her years of obsessive isolation and bereavement following Albert's death tried her public's patience, prompting some to suggest that she abdicate.

Victoria riding in an open carriage in the mid-1860s. The queen's return to public life and ceremonial function was gradual and tentative, but, cheered by a populace quite ready for her resumption of queenly duties, Victoria began to rediscover her passion for living.

THE BETTMANN ARCHIVE

Queen Victoria unveils the Albert Memorial Statue in Edinburgh. The statue was one of many tributes erected throughout Great Britain to commemorate her beloved husband; one of Victoria's favorites was Albert's mausoleum, where she went often to grieve and contemplate.

tinue her duties, although on a very minimal level. In the early period of her bereavement, she would not even see her ministers, using her daughter Princess Alice as a go-between instead. When required to attend a meeting of the Privy Council, she remained in a separate room where she could hear the proceedings, but could not be seen. Similarly, she attended church by entering the side chapel from a special entrance, and sat beyond the view of the congregation. These brief forays into public places required a tremendous amount of emotional discipline from Victoria; she adopted a rigid exterior in order to maintain some sense of composure. Invariably, her grief would overwhelm her the moment she returned home.

The queen's primary objective during this period

Otto von Bismarck (1815–98), the Prussian statesman whose militaristic policies helped create the German empire in 1871. Bismarck's ambitions led to hostility between Victoria and her daughter Vicky (who had married the Prussian crown prince) and to the wars for supremacy in continental Europe.

of loss was not to recover, but to sustain and perpetuate Albert's memory. Her pursuit of this objective was obsessive. For instance, his room at Osborne was photographed so that every detail might be preserved just the way he had kept it. His nightshirt was laid out every evening. His portrait hung over his pillow, as well as the pouch in which he used to keep his watch during the night. A visitor to Osborne can still see them there today.

Victoria covered the landscape with memorials to her beloved husband. Statues and commemorative stones were erected all over Britain. And finally, the Victoria Memorial in Kensington Gardens was opened in 1872. England would not forget the deeds and sterling character of Albert the Good — not if Victoria could help it.

The queen also had a mausoleum constructed for Albert at Frogmore near Windsor, where she too planned to be laid to rest. This structure became more than his place of interment; it became the home of her grief as well. The cold silent rooms of the mausoleum became one of her favorite retreats, a place where she would go to pray or simply sit and gaze upon his tomb.

As Victoria mourned the death of her husband, events were transpiring on the European continent that would soon demand her attention. King William I of Prussia had appointed Otto von Bismarck as his chief minister in September 1862, an appointment that Prussian Crown Prince Frederick and his wife (Victoria's daughter Vicky) had strongly opposed. The Prussian statesman wanted to unify the various German states and make them independent of Austria. He declared that great political questions would be decided not by "speeches and resolutions of majorities . . . but by blood and iron." Bismarck and his militaristic policies were catching on, however, and the young couple's strident resistance made them so unpopular that they decided to withdraw from public life. Bismarck, meanwhile, enjoyed the confidence and support of the German people as he plotted an aggressive course for Prussia, one that would eventually lead his nation to challenge Austria for supremacy in Europe.

Oh how fearful it is, to be suspected—uncheered—unguided and unadvised—and how alone the poor Queen feels.
—QUEEN VICTORIA
writing to Lord Granville

One of the opening clashes that resulted from this wave of Prussian adventurism involved the two Danish duchies of Schleswig and Holstein, which bordered on Prussia. The king of Denmark had died and several opposing claims of ownership regarding these states began to arise. The legal intricacies of their contest had a long and complicated history, one that Lord Palmerston claimed only three people had ever understood: Prince Albert, who was now dead, a German professor who had gone mad, and he himself — who had now forgotten the details. It was clear however, that the strongest rivalry was between the claims laid by Prussia and Denmark.

Victoria was deeply upset by this heated debate, because she had children and relatives on both sides of it. Her son Bertie's new wife, Alexandra, was grief-stricken by the death of her father, the Danish king, and was distressed by the cold-blooded aggressiveness of the Prussians. Simultaneously, her eldest daughter Vicky was in Prussia and made furious accusations against Britain. Victoria, torn

Helena (1846–1923), Victoria's fifth child. The princess married Prince Christian (1798–1869) of Schleswig-Holstein, which was invaded by the Prussians in 1864 as part of Bismarck's empire-building.

Beatrice (1857–1944), Victoria's ninth and final child. Beatrice married Prince Henry of Battenberg (1858–96) and was the mother of Queen Victoria Eugenia of Spain (1887– 1969).

by love, remained sympathetic to the Prussian cause, largely because she believed it to be what Albert would have wished. However, the situation regarding the right of succession within the duchies had changed considerably since Albert's death, and perhaps he would have sided with the Danish against the Prussians.

Pressures over this debate continued to mount, and when Princess Alexandra gave birth to a premature son, these pressures were thought to be largely responsible. The infant was of delicate health, and the English people were greatly saddened by this misfortune. Bertie and Alexandra had always enjoyed immense popularity among the British, who now held Prussia to be largely responsible for their sorrows.

In 1864 Prussian armies swept into both Schleswig and Holstein. Victoria, who had been willing to support Prussia diplomatically, was outraged by this bold and arrogant invasion. Her letter to Vicky was frank and expressed her disdain of what she felt was an act of betrayal, adding "God forgive you for it." Victoria expected that after the Danish had been defeated, the Prussians would withdraw and resume their diplomatic campaign. Bismarck had other ideas, however: He intended to build a mighty nation, and now that he held the disputed land, he was determined to keep it. Despite some saber-rat-

> *The great worry and anxiety and hard work for ten years, alone, unaided, with increasing age and never very strong health almost drove the Queen to despair.*
> —QUEEN VICTORIA
> of the 10 years following Albert's death

Arthur (1850–1942), Victoria's seventh child and third son, in military regalia. He became the duke of Connaught, and his daughter Margaret (1882–1920) married King Gustav VI of Sweden (1882–1973).

tling by Lord Palmerston in a speech before the House of Commons, Britain took no military steps to oppose Bismarck. Two years later, Bismarck defeated Austria in seven weeks, and created the independent North German Confederation.

Victoria struggled to fulfill her obligations as queen. The dispatch boxes continued to pour in, demanding judgments, responses, and opinions. Meanwhile, the public's patience with Victoria's extended mourning began to wear thin. At first, her subjects had made their queen's grief their own, their sympathy for her loss being the uppermost

Victoria in 1863 with her Scottish servant John Brown. After Albert's death, Brown became the queen's confidant and helped to restore her enthusiasm.

Princess Victoria and her husband, German Emperor Frederick III of Prussia (1831—88). Vicky denounced Britain during a Prussian-Danish territorial dispute in the 1860s, causing Queen Victoria much anguish. Vicky's eldest son, William II (1859—1941), was the German kaiser during World War I.

feeling in their hearts. But her continued refusal to perform many of her duties attracted increasing criticism, particularly from the press.

The queen claimed that her subjects had no understanding of the enormous amount of desk work that occupied her. While this was true, Victoria also found public duties overwhelming — probably because she feared that her rigidly composed veneer might break. Her protests and excuses satisfied neither the press nor her subjects, who felt that a monarch has a public duty to be visible to her people. She did not have the freedom or the right to continue to indulge in a private sorrow that estranged her from her subjects. It began to be suggested that she abdicate in favor of her popular son, Bertie, the Prince of Wales.

Victoria clung to her grief with an almost desperate tenacity. For a while, she resorted to subterfuge

Victoria in the early 1870s. By this time the queen was beginning to shed her grief and reassert herself in affairs of state.

SNARK/ART RESOURCE

in order to avoid public appearances, claiming that ill health and shattered nerves made such appearances impossible. Although her claims were invariably supported and confirmed by doctors' statements, her subjects continued to demand her presence.

At long last, almost exhausted by the controversy her seclusion had caused, she began to reemerge very slowly into the public eye. Also, as time wore on, she had begun to regain confidence in her own abilities, no longer feeling that the only way to honor Albert's memory was to emulate him.

Victoria's public appearances began to increase, although not often enough to appease public demand. Her subjects enthusiastically welcomed her back on these occasions, such as on June 1, 1864, when she drove out in an open carriage and found a cheering crowd ready to greet her. These demonstrations of affection warmed Victoria's heart and helped to ease her back into her public duties.

Her return from seclusion was also aided by a new and somewhat unlikely friend, her Scottish manservant John Brown. Brown became attached to the royal retinue during early sojourns to the Highlands, where Albert had made the original suggestion that Victoria take him as a personal servant while at Balmoral. His loyalty and courage were above reproach, as he had proven by saving the queen from several riding accidents.

In 1864, on the advice of her doctors, Victoria decided to begin riding again and was persuaded to summon Brown to become her personal groom. He arrived in winter of that year and quickly became indispensable to her. Not only did she place great trust in his simple country wisdom and brusque goodness, but he reminded her of the earlier, happier days at Balmoral. His presence made Albert seem closer, more tangible. Between these associations and his own solid qualities, Brown proved to be a source of welcome reassurance to Victoria, whom he made the focus of all his attentions. She responded in kind, becoming very attached to the big Scotsman, who became more a friend than a servant.

On some occasions, her fondness for Brown annoyed the rest of the household, including her children. As Victoria's personal servant, no one else was permitted to give him orders. He accompanied her everywhere, was given access to her room, and was often the only channel through which people could communicate with the queen.

Victoria was obstinate, particularly when her ministers expressed the desire that she exclude Brown from accompanying her on public appearances. Once again, Victoria's passionate sense of dedication and loyalty flared up, and she began to perceive any slight to Brown as a slight to herself. She refused to alter the situation, responding, "The Queen will not be dictated to."

Rumors began to spring up which suggested that she and Brown were secretly married. Despite these malicious tales, the queen's relationship with Brown was largely unchanged until his death many years later. While their friendship was certainly unorthodox — and for some members of the royal family quite embarrassing — it nonetheless proved to be the best antidote to Victoria's misery. With Brown's help, she gradually overcame her sense of despondency and rediscovered her interest in life.

malicious

THE BETTMANN ARCHIVE

Victoria listens as a servant reads her the newspaper.

95

6

She Reigns Alone: Victoria Victorious

She was the greatest of all Englishwomen—I had almost said of Englishmen.
—JOSEPH CHAMBERLAIN
British statesman

In 1866 some of Victoria's energy and enthusiasm returned. It was in that year that the Conservative party came into office and that Benjamin Disraeli was appointed both chancellor of the exchequer and leader of the House of Commons. In accordance with these new positions, Disraeli began to communicate directly with the queen, informing her of the daily events in the House of Commons. These were not the dry accounts to which Victoria had become accustomed, but lively, informative, amusing essays that brought the parliamentary scene to life. The queen's desk work, always the trial of her existence, suddenly grew brighter and more enjoyable.

Disraeli, or "Dizzie" as he was called, was nearing the end of a long political career, which he had further augmented by being a successful author. His novel *Sybil* depicted the exploitative methods used by mining companies to take earnings from the miners they employed. However, his initial encounters with the queen had not been particularly successful. The first instance in which he attracted royal attention was his opposition to Sir Robert Peel,

Tsar Nicholas II (1868–1918) and Victoria's granddaughter Tsarina Alexandra (1872–1918) with their daughter Olga and Queen Victoria. In 1877 Victoria was made empress of India, giving her equal status with the imperial rulers of Russia, Austria, and Germany.

THE BETTMANN ARCHIVE

Benjamin Disraeli (1804–81) twice served Queen Victoria as prime minister, in 1868 and 1874–80. He came to power as founder of the modern Conservative party, won Victoria's favor, and pursued aggressive, imperialistic policies.

the Tory prime minister who had earned the admiration and affection of both Victoria and Albert. Disraeli had opposed the bill for the repeal of the Corn Laws, and thereby was largely responsible for splitting Peel's party and bringing about his fall from government. In those earlier days, Victoria had been less than pleased with Disraeli's flamboyant taste in clothes and his brash manner. Albert's disapproval was even stronger, causing him to state bluntly that Disraeli "had not one single element of a gentleman in his composition."

In spite of these unfortunate first impressions, Disraeli eventually won Victoria's favor. She soon discovered his warmth, wit, and sympathy. Moreover, he was the catalyst that brought her back to public life with a revitalized zest for government.

From 1868 to 1893, the two chief protagonists on the parliamentary scene were Disraeli, spokesman for the Conservative party, and William Gladstone, head of the Liberal party. Their positions as party leaders were all that they had in common; in every other perceivable way they were complete opposites.

Unlike Disraeli, Gladstone had earned Albert's warmest approval in the earlier years. He had begun his parliamentary career as a disciple of Sir Robert Peel, and since that time had been a constant opponent of the more engaging and witty Disraeli. Victoria agreed with Albert that Gladstone was an admirable and eminently moral man, but she could not bring herself to like him. Unlike Disraeli, he could not deal with Victoria on a personal level, but only as a symbol to be admired and revered. It is ironic that it was because of his tremendous respect for the queen that he was unable to endear himself to her in any way; the extremity of his deference made his behavior stiff and awkward. During the course of his successive ministries, he and the queen grew further and further apart until, in the end, she felt nothing but antipathy for this well-meaning man.

When Lord Derby resigned as prime minister in 1868, Disraeli was called upon to fill the post for the first time in his long parliamentary career. When he came before Victoria to receive the appointment, he

> *He speaks to me as if I were a public meeting.*
> —QUEEN VICTORIA
> writing about Gladstone

William Gladstone (1809–98), leader of the Liberal party and prime minister four times between 1868 and 1894. Though Queen Victoria called him "that dreadful old man," and despite an abrasive personality, Gladstone enacted a far-reaching and much-needed series of social reforms.

requested, in his characteristic style, that she would "deign not to withhold from him the benefit of your Majesty's guidance." His first term of office was destined to be a short one, yet he and Victoria established a strong bond of affection and respect.

Disraeli and the Conservatives succeeded in passing the second Reform Bill of 1867, an act which gave the vote to an unprecedented number of workingmen. Nonetheless, a wave of fervent republicanism began to sweep the country and the public clamored for more radical reform than the Conservatives were willing to deliver. The Conservatives were badly defeated in the general elections of 1869, when Gladstone and his Liberals swept the ballot.

With Gladstone as prime minister, it soon became evident that Victoria's displeasure with him was not simply personal, but political as well. For the next five years, Britain's Liberal government passed a virtual flood of reforms. Many of these changes, particularly those that affected the army and the navy, were completely contrary to Victoria's personal wishes, but no matter how she complained, she was powerless to stop them.

As if adding insult to injury, Gladstone's personal demeanor, and even his writing style, were sources of constant annoyance to the queen. His explanations were lengthy, pedantic, and, to Victoria, totally incomprehensible. She angrily wrote, "he speaks to me as if I were a public meeting."

However, her friendship with Disraeli continued to grow, even though he was out of office. This was somewhat reminiscent of that earlier period when she had continued her relationship with Melbourne once Sir Robert Peel had replaced him. Victoria found Disraeli's letters a constant source of interest and delight, filled with wry wit and double-edged rhetoric. Before long, they were regularly exchang-

London poor, 1908. As the monarchy's power lessened toward the end of the 19th century, Queen Victoria turned again to humanitarian concerns, establishing a Royal Commission on Housing and publicizing the need for adequate medical care for the working class.

ing tokens of affection. She sent him primroses, which she had gathered from the grounds of Osborne; he sent her a set of his novels. Not to be outdone, she returned the gesture by sending him a copy of her privately published *Leaves from the Journal of Our Life in the Highlands*. After this exchange, he was often heard starting his statements to the queen with the phrase, "we authors, ma'am," which clearly delighted her.

In 1870 Bismarck's Prussian forces were again on the move — this time against France. Britain was then less afraid of the Prussians than of the French. Victoria found reason to declare that the Prussians represented the side "of civilization, of liberty, of order and of unity."

Late in 1871 Victoria had to deal with an event that at last made her completely forget her own woes. As the tenth anniversary of Albert's death was approaching, she received word that Bertie, the Prince of Wales, had fallen seriously ill with typhoid — the same disease that had killed his father.

The crown prince had not been close to his mother for quite some time. Victoria had secretly held him responsible for Albert's death, believing that if Bertie had not become involved in his scandal with the actress, Albert would never have had to journey to Cambridge, wear himself out, and ultimately contract typhoid. Victoria had added to the rift that began to grow between them by renewing all her old criticisms of him, comparing him unfavorably to his father. She refused to allow him into her confidence concerning matters of state, and permitted him to see only brief synopses of the dispatches. It may well have been that there was more than Victoria's resentment at work here; she may have feared that he might oppose her regarding certain public affairs. Whatever the reasons, Victoria rejected her prime ministers' suggestions that the prince be given a more significant place in the royal government. Victoria, temperamental as always, insisted on reinforcing her own attitudes and opinions. She had come to feel that Bertie was simply not truly competent or a hard enough worker — and so, she managed to prevent him from having the opportu-

Is there not just a risk in encouraging her in too large ideas of her personal power and too great indifference to what the public expects?
—LORD DERBY
British statesman,
speaking about Victoria

nity to disprove either of these beliefs by denying him any involvement in things of importance.

In actuality, Bertie had overcome many of his earlier difficulties and had matured into an extremely capable young man, possessed of many talents and an extensive knowledge of the modern world. He realized that the world was changing and that the old order had to change with it if disaster were to be averted. His advice and opinions were sought after by many, and he moved freely in all circles of society. This contrasted sharply with Victoria's narrower, courtbound world, where she often failed or refused to see that times and the people who made them were changing. Also, largely because of Albert's example, she insisted on a strict moral code and impeccable behavior, and therefore it was only natural that she disapproved of the fashionable social life the Prince of Wales enjoyed.

However, when Bertie fell ill in 1871, all these objections and differences that Victoria felt evaporated instantly. The only thing that she thought about was Bertie's health, remarking that this "one great anxiety seems to absorb everything else." At first word of his sickness, she went immediately to his home at Sandringham. Finding him better, she returned to Windsor, only to learn that he had had another relapse and was once again gravely ill. Without hesitation, she turned about and rushed back to his bedside.

It was a trying siege for them both, but on December 15, Victoria's worst fears were dispelled; the crown prince rallied and gave his mother a kiss. In that one instant, years of doubt and suspicion were washed away and Victoria rejoiced in her free, new-found love for her son.

To mark the occasion, Bertie and the queen attended a service of thanksgiving at St. Paul's in February 1872. As they entered together, they received thunderous applause. The people were not only overjoyed at Bertie's recovery, but delighted at Victoria's apparent rejuvenation. Despite her previous seclusion, Victoria had raced to his side to keep watch over him and weather the ordeal with him as only a mother could. The nation's sympathy for her

Disraeli's audacious magic, though not of a kind to transform a neurotic widow into an unimpeachable, sober figurehead, lifted the monarchy out of the trough which was its greatest danger.
—LYTTON STRACHEY
British historian,
describing Disraeli's effect
on Victoria

also began to revitalize the old love with which her subjects had regarded her.

Two days later, while she was driving in her carriage, there was an attempt on her life. The British people were enraged at the assault and through that rage, came once again to appreciate the grand queen they had so nearly lost. Victoria's reconciliation with her people was complete; she had recovered the affection and loyalty of her people.

By 1874 Victoria and Disraeli were ready to resume their political work together. The republican enthusiasm had diminished and Disraeli returned as the head of a new Conservative government. He was then 70 years old.

Victoria was of course delighted to welcome back her favorite minister. The personal quality of their friendship and their basic agreement over policy matters quickly replaced the lack of harmony that had typified the queen's previous five years dealing with Gladstone. The business of government was once again a pleasure for Victoria, particularly since Disraeli not only kept her completely informed, but sought her advice in a great many matters.

Others but herself may submit to his [Gladstone's] democratic rule but not the Queen.
—QUEEN VICTORIA
to Sir Henry Ponsonby,
April 4, 1880

Disraeli had an aggressive style when it came to foreign affairs, pursuing a course that was both adventurous and imperialistic. Victoria shared Disraeli's predeliction for this sort of diplomacy, and in one instance was the actual instigator of a major change in foreign policy. The queen had not forgotten Disraeli's earlier suggestions regarding India, and was now ready to act on them — she wanted to become empress of India.

Europe already boasted three emperors: the tsar of Russia, the emperor of Austria, and the emperor of Germany (the title that young Vicky's husband Frederick was one day to inherit). The queen's lively and romantic imagination painted grand mental pictures of herself as the benign and mighty empress of the teeming subcontinent of India. Her ambition was firm — she and England should not be left out of this current rage of imperial title-making.

It fell to Disraeli to make this dream a reality, and as he expected, this was easier said than done. When he announced the Royal Titles Bill in Parliament (which granted the queen the title of empress of India), it was angrily attacked. But as always, Disraeli was persistent and persuasive, and finally succeeded in getting the bill passed. A more substantive achievement was his buying out Egypt's share in the Suez Canal, which connected the Mediterranean and the Red seas. He obtained the necessary capital in 1873 from the Rothschild bankers, whom he knew. In the 1870s more than half the shipping on the high seas was British; more than half the tonnage that passed through the "lifeline to India" was British. Now Disraeli had secured ownership of the canal for Britain. Victoria rewarded his efforts by making him earl of Beaconsfield. Though Victoria never visited most of her imperial holdings, she was proclaimed empress in 1877.

While Victoria's installment as empress of India was perhaps the most grandiose of England's imperialistic policies, it was certainly not an isolated example. The imperialism that typified Disraeli's ministry reflected the attitude of the British public; theirs was a powerful appetite for conquest and dominion, as was expressed in one popular song of those times:

> We don't want to fight but by jingo if we do
> We've got the ships, we've got the men
> We've got the money too

This song not only typified the tenor of the times, but gave it a name — *jingoism* — which became synonymous with the imperialistic aggressiveness that was sweeping the Western world in general and Britain in particular.

The inspiration for the song was the Russo-Turkish War of 1877, and the international pressures that accompanied it. This time, however, the cause of the hostilities was not as clear-cut as in the Crimean War. Revolts had broken out in Turkey's Balkan provinces, specifically those that bordered Russia. Turkey accused Russia of inciting these rebellions, and moved troops into the troubled areas, suppressing the revolts but also slaughtering thou-

There is a transparency in Victoria's truth that is very striking—not a shade of exaggeration in describing feelings or facts; like very few other people I ever knew. Many may be as true, but I think it goes often with some reserve. She talks all out; just as it is; no more and no less.

—LADY LYTTELTON
governess to
Victoria's children

sands of Bulgarian Christians. European powers were stunned by the massacres and attempted to restrain Turkey through diplomatic channels — without success.

In Britain, Gladstone denounced the Turks as the obvious aggressors, whereas Victoria and Disraeli played down the Turkish atrocities, maintaining that Britain had to support its old ally from the Crimean War. Russia was a potential foe that engendered fear and suspicion in the British people, their queen in particular. War with Russia was not only very possible, but likely to be very costly in both money and lives — a worry that the lyrics of the jingoist glossed over.

Fortunately, war was averted, largely through the brilliant work of Disraeli at the Congress of Vienna. He was able to arrange a peaceful solution through a complicated set of diplomatic maneuvers, an achievement that was to be remembered as one of his greatest triumphs.

Guglielmo Marconi (1874–1937). His invention of the wireless telegraph in 1895 broke vast new ground in world communication. Marconi's Wireless Telegraph Company sent signals across the English Channel between France and England in 1898, and then across the Atlantic Ocean to the United States in 1901.

However, not all of Disraeli's imperialist adventures were so glowingly successful. His attempts to add Afghanistan to the empire failed, leading to the massacre of the British mission in that country in 1879. Gladstone took the opportunity to rail against Disraeli's policies, which he considered extravagant and overly aggressive.

Despite — or perhaps, because of — the seesaw swings of policy and events during this period, Victoria never found her political duties dull. The stakes were always high and the tempo was quick. She was greatly disappointed when Disraeli's ministry ended in 1880, and when ill health removed him from politics entirely a short time later. He died in 1881.

The queen was less than pleased with his successor, Lord Gladstone. He and his two successive Liberal governments proved to be an ever increasing annoyance to Victoria, who had been angered by Gladstone's position during the Russo-Turkish War. As the months passed, she was unable to follow her constitutional duty to ignore party prejudices.

Cecil Rhodes (1853–1902), English imperialist and financier, in South Africa. Rhodes made a fortune as owner of the world's leading diamond mine and then used his power to extend British rule in the region. Though his political fortunes later plummeted, his private monies have since been used to fund "Rhodes scholars" to study at Oxford University.

She could not sympathize or agree with Gladstone at all, and the prime minister was forced to put as much distance between them as his office would allow. Besides his troubles with the queen, Gladstone had also inherited from Disraeli a number of extremely difficult problems in foreign policy ranging from secessionist movements in South Africa to the expansion of the empire's hold in northeastern Africa.

During the latter half of the 19th century, Britain controlled Egypt and her possessions. In 1881, the southern colony of Sudan rebelled and drove out Egyptian occupation forces. In order to regain control, Britain sent troops under the command of the famous Charles George "Chinese" Gordon — a name acquired during the suppression of the Taiping Rebellion (1863–64). In 1884 the British troops captured the Sudan, a country in east central Africa. Soon afterwards, Gordon was under siege by native forces and in desperate need of support. Victoria and her subjects wanted to send more forces immediately, but Gladstone delayed. He finally dispatched a relief force, but it arrived two days too late — the valiant garrison and its commander, General Gordon, had been slaughtered. Victoria's dislike of Gladstone took on a new and intense vehemence. She was never to forgive him for his indecisiveness and for the horrible loss of life that it had caused.

Gladstone served one more term as prime minister before finally retiring, a term marked by more bitterness between himself and the queen. Their meetings were always polite but cold, and sometimes Victoria refused to see him at all. Right up to his last day in office, Gladstone was profoundly disappointed that he had never been able to secure her support and friendship.

Victoria got along well with all her subsequent ministers, largely because none of them aroused either the affection she had felt for Disraeli or the disdain she had felt for Gladstone. Also, her interest in politics had begun to wane. Victoria was growing old, and so was her form of government. The monarchy she had ascended to in 1838 had undergone

No it is better not. She would only ask me to take a message to Albert.
—BENJAMIN DISRAELI replying, in April 1881, to the suggestion that the Queen visit him in his last illness

This German cartoon depicts the supposedly typical British predilection for evangelism on the one hand and imperialism on the other.

many fundamental changes: powers had been redefined, the voting franchise had been expanded, and numerous reforms had changed the shape of government and society. It was a different world, and she as queen had become much less essential to the processes of government.

Victoria shifted her interest back to the humanitarian concerns that she had inherited from Albert. Her return from seclusion had been marked by a new and deeper sympathy for the great numbers of her subjects who spent their lives in abject poverty and misery.

Her primary interest was in plans to improve housing for the poor, and in 1884 a Royal Commission on Housing was appointed. Also, as a result of her contact with Florence Nightingale, she maintained a keen interest in hospitals and medical care for the working class. Victoria's concern for the conditions of the less fortunate led to controversial visits, such as trips to a workhouse in Windsor, and due to her compassion for outcasts of her own sex, the Parkhurst Prison for Women.

Although Victoria showed great sympathy toward other women during her long reign, and was herself one of the world's most powerful women, she was hardly an advocate of women's rights. In 1870, after receiving reports on the women's suffrage movement, she wrote, "The Queen is most anxious to enlist everyone who can speak or write to join in checking this mad, wicked folly of 'Woman's Rights,' with all its attendant horrors, on which her poor feeble sex is bent, forgetting every sense of womanly feeling and propriety."

Victoria's last years were happy ones, and her reign ended on a note of success and triumph. She appeared at many public gatherings and was greeted by cheering crowds on those occasions. She had become more than a queen; she had become an institution, a living definition of what a monarch could and should be.

The fiftieth year (1887) of her reign signalled the celebration of her Golden Jubilee, a magnificent affair that attracted kings and various royalty from all over the world. The event overflowed with colorful pageantry, and was highlighted by a huge royal procession to Westminster Abbey, through the streets of London. At the cathedral, Victoria was once again enthroned — but her thoughts were with Albert, wishing that he could have been there beside her.

The day's festivities included banquets, parades and presentations, and finally concluded in a dazzling fireworks display late that night. In order to adequately honor the queen and empress, London celebrated the jubilee for a month.

Like others who reach so advanced an age, Victoria, aware of how many of her loved ones had died, became increasingly aware of her own mortality. The next decade saw her involvement and interest in affairs of state slacken and virtually disappear.

> *Her [Victoria's] court was pure; her life serene; / God gave her peace; her land repose; / A thousand claims to reverence closed / In her as Mother, Wife and Queen.*
> —ALFRED LORD TENNYSON
> quoted from his poem
> "To The Queen"

Horatio Herbert, Lord Kitchener (1850–1916), British military leader. Kitchener served in Egypt during Britain's occupation of that country in 1882 and in the Sudan in 1884–85 when British forces tried (but failed) to relieve General Charles Gordon (1833–85), who was besieged at Khartoum by rebellious Sudanese.

Queen Victoria on one of her four visits to Ireland. Victoria's relations with the Irish were somewhat ambivalent. Though she admired the Irish, she was firmly against Irish "home rule," which she saw as disloyalty.

From my heart I thank my beloved people. May God bless them!

—QUEEN VICTORIA
message to her subjects,
night of the Jubilee of 1897

On the occasion of her Diamond Jubilee (which took place in 1897, when Victoria had ruled for 60 years), she received her guests in a wheelchair, and the ceremonies were kept brief in deference to her age — she was now 79 years old. But it was nonetheless a magnificent affair, and Victoria was still a clever conversationalist and an imposing monarchical presence. This time the invitations included not only all the crowned heads of Europe (a great many of whom were relatives), but representatives of all her colonies. During the affair, Victoria was invited to use the newly developed telegraph. She tapped out a message that sped throughout the empire in seconds: "From my heart I thank my beloved people. May God bless them."

On January 13, 1901, Victoria made no entry in the journal she had kept faithfully since she was 13. A bulletin from Buckingham Palace informed her subjects that the queen was failing rapidly, and England solemnly waited for the end. Her children and grandchildren flocked to Osborne House, where, on January 22, she died in their midst.

But the image and the ideals of Victoria have proved powerful and enduring throughout history. As the longest reigning monarch in the history of Britain, she had become the symbol of an age — a firm, solitary figure, who personified duty, conscience, morality, and stability.

Victoria had restored dignity and respectability to the English throne, and gave it a new sense of majesty and grace as well. She had seen the monarchy change with the times, its power curtailed and altered as industrialization and republicanism became the dominant forces in British society. But she had not viewed those changes as heralding the defeat of the monarchy; rather, she had worked to shape a new role for that old institution. Victoria had separated the crown from party politics, and had given it a sense of prestige that made it the heart and soul of the people, the place they looked to for calm in crisis, strength in war, compassion amidst tragedy. Victoria had brought monarchy into the modern age, and in that achievement, she was unmatched.

Queen Victoria's funeral, January 1901. Her body was laid to rest beside Prince Albert's in the mausoleum at Frogmore, near Windsor. She was eulogized as a popular queen who had restored dignity to the throne and brought the monarchy into the modern age.

Further Reading

Bradford, Sarah. *Disraeli.* New York: Stein & Day, 1982.

Duff, David. *Victoria in the Highlands: The Personal Journal of Her Majesty Queen Victoria.* Taplinger Publishing Co., 1969.

Henkels, Marie L. *Victoria.* New York: Woodhill Press, Inc., 1979.

Inge, William R. *The Victorian Age.* Darby, Pennsylvania: Arden Library, 1978.

Morley, John. *The Life of William Ewart Gladstone* (3 vols.) New York: Greenwood Press, 1968.

Strachey, Lytton. *Queen Victoria.* New York: Harcourt, Brace & World, 1921.

Thomson, David. *England in the Nineteenth Century.* New York: Penguin Books, 1978.

Whittle, Tyler. *Victoria and Albert at Home.* London: Routledge & Kegan Paul, Ltd., 1980.

Woodham-Smith, Cecil. *Queen Victoria: From Her Birth to the Death of the Prince Consort.* New York: Alfred A. Knopf, Inc., 1972.

Chronology

May 24, 1819	Born Alexandrina Victoria, the daughter of Edward, the duke of Kent, and Victoria, the princess of Saxe-Coburg, at Kensington Palace
Jan. 23, 1820	The duke of Kent dies
Jan. 29, 1820	George III, king of Great Britain, dies; succeeded by George IV
June 1830	King George IV dies and is succeeded by William IV
June 20, 1837	King William IV dies Victoria accedes to the throne of Great Britain
June 28, 1838	Crowned at Buckingham Palace
May 1839	Refuses to remove her Whig chambermaids—in an incident known as the "Bedchamber Crisis"—after Tory party elected to power
Feb. 10, 1840	Marries Prince Albert of Saxe-Coburg-Gotha in the chapel at St. James's Palace
1841–46	Sir Robert Peel serves as prime minister
1846	In an attempt to relieve famine in Ireland and England, Parliament repeals the Corn Laws, which restricted importation of grain Lord Russell becomes prime minister
May 1, 1851	Victoria officially opens the Great Exhibition, a display of the newest developments in British art, science, and technology
1854–56	Britain, France, and Turkey fight Russia in the Crimean War Victoria organizes relief for wounded British troops
1858	Victoria and her government assume full control of India—under the New India Bill—after native troops rebel against the East India Company
1855–65	Lord Palmerston serves—except for one brief interval—as prime minister
1861	Prince Albert helps to avert war with the U.S. and to gain release of Confederate envoys who had been captured by the Union from the British vessel *Trent*
Dec. 14, 1861	Prince Albert dies
1861–64	Victoria mourns Albert's death and retreats from public view
1864	Appoints John Brown as her personal groom
1868–74	William E. Gladstone heads Liberal administration
1874–80	Benjamin Disraeli heads Conservative administration
1877	Victoria is proclaimed empress of India
1884	Creates Royal Commission on Housing to secure housing for the poor
1887	Celebrates Golden Jubilee, marking the 50th year of her reign
1897	Celebrates Diamond Jubilee, marking the 60th year of her reign
Jan. 22, 1901	Victoria dies, aged 81, at the Osborne House

Index

Deirdre Shearman was born in the British Isles and educated in England, Switzerland and the United States, where she has lived since 1959. She is the mother of three sons. Her principle historical interest is the British Raj in India.

Arthur M. Schlesinger, jr., taught history at Harvard for many years and is currently Albert Schweitzer Professor of the Humanities at City University of New York. He is the author of numerous highly praised works in American history and has twice been awarded the Pulitzer Prize. He served in the White House as special assistant to Presidents Kennedy and Johnson.